A PARENT'S GUIDE FOR EDUCATIONAL SUCCESS
FOR THEIR CHILDREN

Joann Falciani

Author's Tranquility Press

Marietta, Georgia

Copyright © 2022 by Joann Falciani

All rights reserved. No part of this publication may be reproduced, distributed or transmitted in any form or by any means, including photocopying, recording, or other electronic or mechanical methods, without the prior written permission of the publisher, except in the case of brief quotations embodied in critical reviews and certain other noncommercial uses permitted by copyright law. For permission requests, write to the publisher, addressed "Attention: Permissions Coordinator," at the address below.

Joann Falciani /Author's Tranquility Press
2706 Station Club Drive SW
Marietta, GA 30060
www.authorstranquilitypress.com

Ordering Information:
Quantity sales. Special discounts are available on quantity purchases by corporations, associations, and others. For details, contact the "Special Sales Department" at the address above.

A Parent's Guide for Educational Success /Joann Falciani
Paperback: 978-1-957208-66-4
eBook: 978-1-957208-67-1

Library of Congress Control Number: 2025923881

Contents

How to Choose the Right School for Your Child 5

How to Choose Kindergarten Placement for your Child 9

Setting a Routine for Children 13

Why you should choose a Healthy School 16

Teach Children to be Grateful about Holidays 20

Benefits of Sports Participation 22

Parent-Teacher Conflict 24

Family Fun and Staying Safe during Halloween 26

Going Through Divorce 29

CHAPTER 1

How to Choose the Right School for Your Child

Is your child joining Elementary or secondary school? No need to worry we will guide you through each step. It is necessary that you choose a school that suits your child's needs.

It might be a tough and stressful process for you but by following our outlined steps you will find it very easy.

There are many options beyond the public school down the street today. This options leave parents in a confused state over how to make the best decision on which learning environment suits their child best. It is important to know what to look for in a school to ensure your child receives the best possible education for his particular needs.

So, how can you verify if a particular school is capable of meeting your needs? We have come up with some factors you should consider when choosing the best school to provide the right education for your child's specific needs;

Type of school

As a parent you know your child the best therefore you have a responsibility to select the type of school where he or she will thrive and grow. Would your child fare best in a traditional school, a Montessori or a religious affiliated school?

You should also ask questions such as is the academic outcome your main goal? Are you interested in a school that focuses on your Child's unique strengths and weaknesses?

Pupil to teacher ratio

A good school should not have an overcrowded classroom; the proper classroom ratios should be one teacher to six kids for two- year-old kids or one teacher to ten children for preschoolers and Kindergarten. Having too many kids to one teacher will limit the amount of attention the teacher can give to pupils, and nothing is more important at that stage than personalized attention from their teacher.

Proper licensing

A great school will be rightly authorized by the Department of Public Welfare for child care hours and the Department of Education for academic activities. You should call both of these departments to find out if there were any violations marked against the school in the past.

Teacher's credentials

You should verify the credentials and qualifications of your kid's teacher; Nearly every state education agency now provides a system that parent's and members of the public can use to check and review the credentials of school teachers in the state.

Make a checklist of relevant questions

> Before visiting the school, you should make a list of some important questions to ask the principals and teachers. Some of the essential questions you should ask include:
> Verify from the Principals about the staff (teacher) turnover rate.
>
> Ask about their illness policy and when children can return to school after being ill.
>
> You should check out the school playground and find out about the duration of time kids spend outside in different seasons and types of weather.
>
> Inquire about progress reports and communication with the teacher.
>
> Ask about preparation for elementary schools.

Talk to other students and parents if possible to find out necessary details as School staffs are known to put their best foot forward while meeting with potential clients.

CHAPTER 2

How to Choose Kindergarten Placement for your Child

As we start to plan for summer camps for our children, we also need to start evaluating the correct placement for our children who are entering kindergarten. It can be tough to choose whether to hold them back or send them to kindergarten. There are many factors that come into play when making this decision.

The child's birthday: For the children whose birthday's fall between June to August 31, it can be a challenging decision. Parents have to meet with the teacher to see where the child is, not only academically but socially. Is your child a self-starter, can compete one and two set directions?

Independent schools will conduct a placement evaluation to know where the child is and whether the child can attain academic success.

Public schools will also conduct an evaluation, but they are very strict about the August 31st deadline

If your children have completed a private school kindergarten, they can enter a public school first grade after the school's evaluation.

Boys and girls develop academically and socially at different levels. Boys can benefit from an additional year in the pre-kindergarten and then kindergarten. As a result of this decision, boys will further develop their self-confidence. Since they will be the oldest in the class, they can become leaders.

Girls can also benefit from an additional year in the pre-kindergarten classroom. If their birthday falls towards the end of the summer, they can enter kindergarten and the teacher will evaluate their progress during the year.

This trend is known as "redshirting." It's a term coined for college football players who maintain an extra year of sports eligibility by practicing with the team as freshmen, but not playing in games. The idea of redshirting preschoolers has blossomed in the wake of a 2006 University of California at Santa Barbara study.

Researchers Kathy Bedard and Elizabeth Dhuey found that grade-schoolers who are among the oldest in their class have a distinct competitive learning edge over the youngest kids in their grade, scoring 4 to 12 percent higher on standardized math and science tests.

CHAPTER 3

Setting a Routine for Children

Children thrive when they have a routine and know what is expected of them. Morning drop-off at preschool, along with pick up can be a tough time of the day for both the child and parents. As adults, we need to include our children in the process.

Here are a few tips:
1) Children should have a healthy breakfast at home before leaving for school. This allows the child to get some energy and prevent eating breakfast at school.
2) Children should carry their own belongings such as backpacks, and lunches to school. Allow children to put away their own belongings. This allows the child to build independence, as well as establishing the routine of drop off.
3) The drop off should be quick. When parents linger at school, the child becomes confused and thinks the parents are staying.
4) There should be either a quick hug, kiss or a wave at the window.
5) Parents should tell the child they will always come back after work.

Model social graces of greeting the teacher in the morning as well as your child greeting the teacher.

Please arrive early. When children arrive late, children can get anxious if they walk in and all the children are looking at them while circle time is being held.

Talk to your child about all the exciting activities that go on at school. Talk about math and playing on the playground. Allow your child to tell you what they love about school.

The teacher can assist with the drop off by greeting the child with a smile and enthusiasm as the child arrives.

Pick up time should have a routine. Children should gather their own belongings and prepare to go home. Parents should have a short chat about their child's day. This is not the time for a parent conference. Teachers are watching other children and can't have lengthy conversations. Parents must refrain from being on the phone during drop off and pick up. Parents should not be distracted by a phone call and should put all their attention on their child and setting them up for a successful day.

The important message is just like adults, children need to know what the expectations are of them, and they will rise to the occasion.

CHAPTER 4

Why you should choose a Healthy School

It's the end of Winter and Spring is approaching, we are reminded that children and teachers are more prone to getting sick with variety odd illnesses which include the flu, strep and common cold.

As a parent, a call from the school can be both frustrating and concerning. You have to leave work and possibly stay home for a couple days.

Here are some tips from a Washington Post Article about keeping everybody healthy:

When a child seems sick or the rash comes on suddenly, a trip to the doctor might be wise, said Linda Davis-Alldritt, a registered nurse and the president of the National Association of School Nurses.

The Common Cold

Stuffy noses, low-grade fevers and coughs are fine as long as the symptoms are mild, the student can do her work and she is not disturbing her classmates.

"By the time symptoms manifest, the child has likely already become contagious," Devore said. "Most kids and teachers are exposed to common viruses, including cold viruses, regularly.

There are enough viruses to have a fresh cold every week and still have a normal immune system."

Influenza

Stay home! Signs that your child has the flu and not a common cold include higher fever, aches and pains, fatigue and severe cough.

"With flu, the fever can be 102 or even higher," Davis-Alldritt said.

"You can look at your kids and you can tell when they are really sick."

Eye discharge

Conjunctivitis, or pink eye, is just that: eye discharge paired with pink or red in the whites of the eyes. It can be caused by a virus or bacteria, or by dust or allergens. The viral and bacterial versions are contagious.

"It's very hard to differentiate between allergic eye irritation and an infection," Davis-Alldritt said. "If as a parent you think it's pinkeye, it's a good idea to call their health-care provider."

Sore throat

Sometimes it's strep. Sometimes it's just irritation from a cold or other respiratory infection. If it's not severe and not accompanied by a significant fever, a child can go to school. If it is strep, she will need to stay home until after she has been on antibiotics for a full day and is feeling better, Devore said. For a viral sore throat, a child should stay home until she has been fever-free for 24 hours.

Vomiting and diarrhea

There's very little gray area here. If your child is throwing up or has diarrhea, the child needs to be picked up from school and kept at home for twenty-four hours. This rule keeps everyone healthy.

Prevention

Kids can prevent many common illnesses with a few simple steps: frequently washing hands for at least 20 seconds with soap and warm water; coughing and sneezing into their elbows; keeping their hands away from their eyes and face; and getting a flu shot and keeping other vaccines up-to-date.

We as educators and parents need to keep everybody healthy and work together for the best interest of the child. The important message is a child doesn't need a fever to be sick.
If the child can't perform in the daily activities at school, he needs to stay home, and receive some medication

CHAPTER 5

Teach Children to be Grateful about Holidays

As I sit in my living room with my tree, lights and wrapping paper. I can't help to think it is truly a magical time of year especially as a teacher of preschoolers. Children are excited in anticipation of Christmas morning and all the magic it brings. Nowadays, Children are also learning to appreciate and embrace several cultures and learn about Hanukkah and Kwanza. We also have a responsibility to teach children the true meaning of Christmas and the joy of giving as well as doing for others.

Here are a few helpful hints to teach children about the joy of the holidays.

1. We can teach children about how to be grateful for everything they have and how they can give to others. Children can help out others, get them involved. Children can go into the community to pass out Christmas cookies and a small message of hope. This will help teach them how to be loving and giving and that the holidays are not all about getting but about helping others.
2. Saint Nicholas Day is a wonderful opportunity to have children choose three or four toys that they don't play with me anymore and give them away to a shelter or a community center.
3. Children can make holiday cards and drawings and visit a senior center to drop them off for the residents.
4. The biggest lesson we can teach children this time of year is about how to make wonderful memories. Spend time with your children and do some fun activities such as:

Bake cookies

Watch a holiday movie as a family with popcorn.

Take a day trip to see Christmas lights Longwood gardens,

Read a holiday book

Make ornaments

CHAPTER 6

Benefits of Sports Participation

We are packing up the beach towels and putting away the bathing suits for the season, fall sports have started for children across the area. Sports have multiple benefits for children on and off the field. Participation in sports can build children's self-esteem as well as their self -confidence. Sports also teaches children goal setting and the importance of following through.

Children gain the following skills:

Social Skills

Sports participation will help children in developing skills that will last a lifetime. They learn to play with children in the same age bracket as well as older children who can act as a role models. Children learn leadership skills, communication and social skills, and grace that they can carry over in their adulthood.

Self-Esteem

Children's self-esteem will increase as they get praise for a job well done. They also learn outshine themselves and reach their athletic potential by the encouragement from coaches. Children also learn to accept constructive criticism which is also an important skill.

School Success

Children who participate in sports excel in academics. They apply the same dedication and hard work on and off the field. Children also are more confident and learn to manage their time better which is a life-long skill.

Health

Children who actively engage in sports also make health food choices. Sports is an excellent way to encourage healthy habit which we should instill in our young ones to carry over to adulthood.

CHAPTER 7

Parent-Teacher Conflict

The relationship between teachers and parents is important to the success of the child at school. Parents will have concerns and issues throughout the school year. Here are some helpful tips to help resolve and navigate these conflicts:

1) In a preschool, drop off and pick up is not always the best time to discuss an in-depth issue with the teacher. Rather, ask for a time to meet or talk during the day that is convenient for both of you.
2) As a parent, you can email the teacher to briefly discuss an issue, but a face to face meeting is more appropriate to resolve an issue.
3) As parents, remember the school and the parents are a team and both want the best for the child.
4) Teachers need to remain objective and use positive words when they discuss the challenges for the child.
5) As a teacher, you need to listen to parents and validate their concern. Parents want to be heard and getting the best for their child is their paramount objective.
6) The parents need to be aware their child is not the only child in the class, and sometimes they should offer advice to the child of how to become a problem solver.

The school and parents are a team who need to work together to provide children with a safe and nurturing environment.

CHAPTER 8

Family Fun and Staying Safe during Halloween

Can you feel it already? Another October 31st is here and Its Halloween season!

Halloween is one of the most exciting and anticipated holidays in the United States, second only to Christmas. It presents such an exciting time for the family to get together for some fun activities; but for the kids, it's like magic in the air! It's that time of the year when they get to wear spooky costumes, enjoy parties and roam the neighborhood looking for treats.

The list of activities for the perfect Halloween must include Family activities and don't forget the ancient tradition of "trick or treat." There are lots of fun activities that the whole family will enjoy on Halloween day, and we have listed a couple of them for you to choose from, any of the activities on this list is guaranteed to give your Halloween celebration a buzz that you won't forget in a long time.

1. Halloween is a great time to go apple picking with the whole family. Who doesn't like apples? You could visit any of the local orchards such as Highland Orchards, Linville orchards or Milky Way Farms. While there, you could also pick pumpkins to carve while munching on some apple cider doughnuts.

2. You could also get some brown or white paper bags to make Halloween lanterns. Just get a small powered tea lamp and a string, and you are good to go!

3. You could design and craft home-made trick or treat bags and also have the children adorn themselves in their Halloween costumes, masks, and paints.

4. You could buy Halloween cookie cutters and have everyone sit around the dining table and make cookies with Halloween themes.

5. Another excellent activity idea is to make Halloween Candy popcorns for the whole family.

6. You could also use the pumpkin seeds to make amazing Halloween crafts like necklaces and paper plates.

7. Later in the evening just before it gets dark, you could all make toilet paper ghosts and put up Halloween decorations

During the evening

As soon as it starts getting dark, it's time for the kids to go out for trick or treat, and in the midst of the euphoria; it is easy for them to let loose and abandon safety precautions. For parents, you can follow these simple tips to keep your children safe during trick or treat:

1. For younger children aged below 7 years, they should be accompanied by at least one adult. For older children, they should go out in pairs.
2. They should follow a planned route and can only go to houses with a well-lit porch.
3. Take care to decorate the kid's costumes and bags with reflective tape or stickers and, if possible, choose light colors as this will increase their visibility in the dark.
4. Endeavor to use paints instead of masks which can obstruct a child's vision and make it harder to see oncoming vehicles.
5. Also, have kids carry glow sticks or flashlights to help them see and be seen by drivers and when selecting a costume, make sure it is the right size to pre- vent trips and falls.

CHAPTER 9

Going Through Divorce

Children are human sponges and will absorb and process information very well when explained in a simple and concise manner. We need to be aware of their ability to process a great deal of information all at once. The subject of divorce is no different and needs to be handled with a great deal of reassurance. They should know that the divorce is not their fault.

Here are some tips to on how to have a discussion with your children about divorce when it occurs:

1. Reassure your children they will still see both parents. Both mom and dad still love them and will always be there for them.
2. They will have two houses where they can play, sleep and have friends over.
3. Parents of young children should maintain routines, provide consistency in rules and expectations, and provide extra affection. Provide young children with repeated reassurances that the divorce is not their fault and that you love them.

Children will ask many questions about the divorce and how it will affect them day to day. Their schedule will change. The child needs to understand that they will spend time with each parent, just not together. As a parent you should seek help from a professional when needed. The professional will be objective, and your children may feel more comfortable talking to a professional, rather than you.

The school is also an important factor in helping children handle divorce and their situation. With so many changes in their schedule, the children will look to the school as a place that provides stability and support. We as educators should listen to the children, but also set limits on behaviors that are acceptable.

We need to let children know that they are valued through our smiles and positive feedback for their efforts as well as their progress. Many children say they do not want to be pitied, but they do want to hear about what they do well. Give them opportunities for leadership and to help the teacher as well as their classmates.

Divorce is a challenge for both the parents and children. Both school and parents need to reassure the children that they are loved and safe. As adults, we need to only say positive qualities about each other because children internalize their feelings and can act based on what they have heard and seen. The best recipe is to make sure children feel safe and loved.

Thank You for Reading Our Book! ©

ABOUT THE AUTHOR

This is where the author biography text goes.
(This page will automatically center vertically.)

Contents

Preface 5
Presentation 7
At The Beginning 9
Sacred and Art 13
From Image to Object 17
Sky and Divinity 20
Sky and Anatomy of Human 26
Examples of Phenomenon 30
Religion, State and Power 45
The Phenomenon of No-Father Birth and Architecture 56
Symbolism and Semiotics 63
Foundation Institution as an Architectural Activity and Symbol 73
Phenomenon of Sacred Birth 77
At The End 81
REFERANCES 84

Muzaffer Yılmaz
Born in Antalya in 1983, Muzaffer Yılmaz studied art history. In 2007, he started his master's degree at Selçuk University Social Sciences Institute, Department of Archeology of the Turkish World and Medieval Cultures, and completed his master's degree in 2010 with his thesis on Historical Water Structures in the Center of Aydın Province; In 2015, he completed his doctorate at Selçuk University Social Sciences Institute, Department of General Art History, with his thesis on Turkish Era Public Buildings I-II in Aydın.

Main areas of work; Yılmaz, who is interested in Mythology and Symbolism, Gastronomy and Art Relationship, Tanzimat Era Turkish Architecture and Urban Aesthetics, works as a faculty member at Konya Necmettin Erbakan University Faculty of Fine Arts.

Published Books:
2018, *Tarihi ve Kültür Varlıkları İle Aydın Güzelhisarı*, Konya: Çizgi Publishing.
2019, *Malatya Lokanta Kültürü ve Hacı Baba Et Lokantası*, Konya: NÜVE Publishing.
2019, *Aydın'da Halkevi Mimarisi*, Konya: Aybil Publishing.
2019, *Osmanlı Sanatında Değişim ve Dönüşüm*, (Editor), Konya: Literatürk-Academia Publishing.

Preface

Even though the popular goals in the academic community are different today, I think; I am of the opinion that thinking and writing, saying new things, and constantly trying even if one cannot achieve results should be the raison d'être of an academician. Especially in these times when we realize that everything can change in an instant and that we cannot actually own anything...

I would like to express my gratitude to our esteemed teacher, Prof. Dr. Selçuk Mülayim, who kindly wrote the introduction of this book, which I finalized on the eve of a transformation, to Prof. Dr. Ahmet Çaycı, who never spared me his support during the writing and publication process, to Assoc. Prof. Dr. Nermin Öztürk, with whom I have consulted many times, whose knowledge I have benefited greatly from, and whose efforts I cannot finish counting, Prof. Dr. Yüksel Göğebakan, who read what I wrote without getting lazy and shared his thoughts with me. I would like to express my gratitude to Associate Professor Fatih Özdemir, to Dr. Lecturer Mehmet Susuz, to Dr. Lect. Binnaz Koca, to Associate Professor Ayşe Budak, To Assoc. Prof. Başak Burcu Eke, to Exp. Erdal Zeki Tomar and Lect. Ahmet Yavuzyılmaz, to Ogulcan Karakoç, who edited the book, and the beautiful person Ismail Çalışkan, the owner of the publishing house.

Konya-2020

Presentation

New ideas in science have always been frightening and sometimes even led to accusations. On the other hand, it is generally accepted that the social sciences of the 21st century must progress with a multidisciplinary approach. Neither art history nor anthropology can stay out of this. For this reason, mythological stories, apocryphal and non-apocryphal ones, and all kinds of belief texts are handled with multifaceted approaches. This expansion of thought is, in the most general sense, something like the removal of immunities.

Researcher Muzaffer Yılmaz's essay titled *The Phenomenon of No-Father Birth* consists of articles brought together to interpret and examine one of the main themes of belief systems. Even the fact that many expert names were consulted, outside of known perspectives and not included in the bibliographies of classical art history books, brings an innovation to the perception of research. Let us state again that even though new perspectives may be subject to accusations, reading Muzaffer Yılmaz, who writes what he thinks honestly and courageously, will be useful and will pave the way for new initiatives.

Prof. Dr. Selcuk Mülayim

At The Beginning

This book you are holding in your hands has emerged[1] as the product of an intellectual adventure of approximately three years. This work, in essence, is a hermeneutical essay on *the sacred and art*, two interrelated phenomena; It is an evaluation in the nature of a trial on the relationship between a *sacred birth*, which has been expressed many times by different researchers in historical, religious, cultural and anthropological terms, and its relationship with art, by reinterpreting it under the name of the *phenomenon of No-Father Birth*. However, I would like to specifically point out that this study is not a *religious* study that falls within the basic field of *theology* and that the mentioned facts are discussed (in the book), centered on *art history*.

In the book, since the main subject of the study is the relationship between sacred births and art, an evaluation has been made through selected examples (specifically the relationship between sky and earth) instead of touching on many different examples from various cultures one by one.

---

1   The subject discussed in the book (in a much narrower framework) was first published in October 2018 as a paper titled The Phenomenon of No-Father Birth and Its Relationship with Art as an Interpretation Attempt from East to West at the 22nd International Medieval and Turkish Period Excavations and Research Center. It was presented at the Art History Research Symposium, but was not published as a text in the proceedings book or any other periodical. For the summary text, see. *Muzaffer Yılmaz (2018)*. "*Doğu'dan Batı'ya Bir Yorumlama Denemesi Olarak Babasız Doğma Fenomeni ve Sanat İlişkisi*", 22. *Uluslararası Ortaçağ ve Türk Dönemi Kazıları ve Sanat Tarihi Araştırmaları Sempozyumu (24-26 Oct. 2019) Summary Book*, İstanbul: MSGSÜ Publishing, p. 162.

Within the scope of the study, many sources from different fields were used, thus trying to expand the meaning and expression of the book.

In the beginning of the book, the definition of the sacred was made depending on its relationship with the first works of art, and then the formation process of a work of art, from its imagination to its creation, was explained with a focus on image-symbol/symbol-object, and the connection between the sacred and art was explained. It has been tried to be justified in relation to the formation process of the work of art. After defining the sacred and art and emphasizing the relationship between them, the divinity of the sky was emphasized and it was questioned whether there was a connection between the change of human anatomy and the sky. Following these general evaluations and determinations about the sacred, art, the sky and humans, examples of the phenomenon in question are given. Following this section, which includes selected examples, first the connection between the phenomenon of no-father birth and the phenomenon of religion and state, and then its formative and guiding mission on architecture is mentioned. After explaining the relationship between the phenomenon of no-father birth and architecture, the relationship between architecture, semiotics and symbolism was mentioned in order to understand the subject better, and in parallel with these narratives, it was questioned whether a connection, albeit indirect, could be established between the foundation culture and the phenomenon of no-father birth. In the last part of the study, a brief evaluation was made on the phenomenon of the holy virgin, based on its relationship with the phenomenon expressed in the book.

In the book consisting of ten chapters, a total of eighteen visuals related to the course of the narration were used. Among the images used in the study, all photographs of works in museums have public domain rights. However, all sources from which the photographs are taken, whether legal or real persons, are also stated in parentheses.

To the orphan children of this country...

It is always the same mysterious scene: the revelation of something "completely different", a reality that does not belong to our world, within objects that are an integral part of our "natural", "profane" world.

Mircea Eliade

Sacred and Art

Ice Age (Paleolithic Period) cave paintings are mentioned (almost without exception) as the oldest works of art in human history in all art history books (Photo 1). Although most of them are animal depictions, there are various theories[2] about the purpose of the paintings, which consist of handprints, furs and stylized human depictions. Despite different opinions, it is generally accepted that these paintings had a magical (belief-related) purpose in terms of the purpose of their creation (Farthing, 2017: 17). This is also valid[3] for female figurines (venuses), another art object of the Ice Age. Leeming and Page state that the productive, nurturing and enlarging properties of the female body constituted a mystery for the people of the

---

2   It is envisaged that these cave paintings, which are claimed to have various requirements such as fear, protection and play, may also have a relationship with gastronomy, provided that they do not break their connection with belief. For detailed information, see Muzaffer Yılmaz (2018). *"An Evaluation on the Origin of Food and Drink Themed Scenes in Western Painting (From the Beginning of the Middle Ages to the End of the Baroque Period)", SDÜ Faculty of Arts and Sciences Journal of Social Sciences*, V: 44, p. 111-138.

3   Primarily, the patterned ostrich eggs found in the Apollo 11 Cave in Southern Namibia (83,000 BC) or the shell beads found in the Blombos Cave in South Africa (77,000 BC) are older than the cave paintings mentioned here. Although cave paintings (and female figurines) are considered the first, they are made in a systematic order in a similar style and are seen in many places.

Ice Age, and depending on this mystery, the statues were made as metaphors of divine beings (Leeming and Page, 2019: 21, 22). It is possible to describe the mystical, magical and mysterious side of these finds, which are generally dated between 30,000 and 10,000 BC, with the word *sacred*. As the meaning of the word sacred; It means[4] something that is loved enough to be worshiped or died for, that requires strong religious respect, and that is divine. Rudolf Otto stated in general terms that the sacred is a rational and intuitive whole and made the following determination:

...The subject expects a different perception than is possible with rational means. The intuitive element is what cannot be perceived conceptually. For this reason, and because language is also a tool of conceptualization, the intuitive element of the sacred is the side on which we cannot formulate any concepts. It is the inexpressible and unspeakable. The concepts we form are based on our sacred experience and are generally dogmatic statements and moral judgments. However, they are not the experience itself, but only its interpretation. This is just a state of perception... (Otto, 2014: 13).

Mircea Eliade considers it necessary to first define holiness in order to define the sacred, and to define sacred phenomena in order to define holiness, and he mentions rites, rituals, myths, hymns, symbols, people, animals, plants and places as sacred phenomena (Eliade, 2014: 27). Fettullah Kalın makes the following inference based on Eliade's findings:

The field of sacred research is the religious person's own life and experience. Everything related to this experience constitutes the field of this research. Sacred books, rites, rituals, myths, architectural structures, monuments, inscriptions, temples and objects are the study objects of this field. (Kalın, 2014: 75).

---

4   TDK.www.tdk.gov.tr/index.php?option=com_gts&arama=gts&guid=TDK.GTS.5d833b32f00d19.30034312. Access Date: 10 August 2019.

It is possible[5] to call the state of perception, intuitive element and religious experience in these determinations as unconscious. In other words, sacred; It can be considered as the perception and comprehension of a creator-god[6] oriented, intuitive

---

5 Based on the findings of both Eliade and Kalın, it is useful to make the following general evaluation regarding the unconscious, religious life, rituals and myths: The sacred is the subject of direct belief as an intuitive awareness focused on the creator-god. Religion can be considered as the institutionalized form of belief. For example, a person can start to believe anything he wants with his free will, he can not care whether there is a contradiction between the things he believes in, and he can stop believing what he believes at any time he wants. Since religion is faced with a set of rules, although there is freedom in choice, it is necessary to be a part of a structure-understanding in practices. It can be said that belief is individual, religion is social. Mythology is a branch of science, and the myths that are its field of study are texts that are considered the oldest sacred stories in human history. Since religion is generally understood as divine-monotheistic religions, it is thought that what is meant by mythology is something different. However, Hinduism and Indian Mythology correspond to the same meaning. It can be said that the confusion here arises from the contradiction between believing and knowing. Coming from the Greek *logos, logic* describes the science of what it comes to an end. Science is a field of activity related to the mind. As mentioned before, *belief-religion-sacred* is intuitive. Therefore, for those who believe in a religion, what that religion tells is the subject of faith (belief), and for those who do not believe, it is the subject of science (mythology). For example, a Muslim, He believes in Hz. Muhammad's Mirac, he has to believe. But a non-Muslim can only see this situation; It examines it within the metaphor of man's ascension to the sky to establish contact with the sacred, considering it as the ascension of the Islamic prophet Muhammad to the sky. He does not see it as a miracle and discusses the event by comparing it with similar examples in history. Therefore, what is meant by religion and what is meant by mythology are ontologically the same. In this respect, the phenomenon we call sacred is related to the same search for meaning by human beings, whether it is the subject of myths or religions.

6 Although the sacred is essentially directly related to god-divinity, in the case of the Ice Age (even though they represent the same phenomenon), it is possible to associate the sacred with concepts-values such as curiosity, fear, sublimity and respect. For the development and change of the idea of God, see. Robert Winston (2010). *The Story of God*, (Trans. Sinan Köseoğlu), Istanbul: Say Publications; Karen Armstrong (2017). *History of God*, (Trans. Oktay Özel, Hamide Koyu¬kan, Kudret Emiroğlu), Istanbul: Pegasus Publications.

awareness related to our unconscious. The concretization of this perception, which is an abstract activity, occurs through objects. For the subject who looks at the object with this eye (or shapes it), the object is a form, a manifestation of its own sacred.

Photo 1: Depiction of an Ice Age Deer, Lascaux Cave, Montignac/ France, Approximately 15,000 BC. (HTO, https://en.wikipedia.org/)

From Image to Object

Beyond many cliché definitions, art is ontologically an imagination-centered expression and a form of indirect expression. In this form of expression, since the artist is fed by imagination in the creation process, the production process; It follows an image-symbol/symbol-object oriented course. The image, defined as a dream conceived in the mind and longed to come true, is the beginning of the interpretation that will come true for the artist. During the design process, the artist transforms the image formed in his mind into an object through symbols[7]. The fact that the perception of art is intuitive and the embodiment process is through signs and symbols makes it necessary for the style of expression to be indirect.

These forms of expression, which can be divided into direct and indirect, are actually related to the way of approaching events or facts. To explain the subject a little more; Terms and concepts that need concrete evidence and cause-effect relationships serve to explain, while imagination, which does not need these at all, helps[8] to make sense[9] of anything. This situation also reveals the differen-

---

7 For the relationship of art with icons and symbols, see. Clare Gibson (2016). *How to Read Symbols*, (Trans. Cem Alpan), Istanbul: YEM Publications.
8 For a seminar recording on the subject, specifically the relationship between imagination and art, see: Dücane Cündioğlu, *Gabriel's Wings, About Imagination*, 15 February 2014. https://www.youtube.com/watch?v=l5P6m-N9a0wk&t=3261s. Access Date: 20 March 2014.
9 In this process of interpretation, gender, age and socio-economic structure come to the fore as important determinants. For detailed information and a scientific study on the relationship between religion and the search for meaning, see. Abdülkerim Bahadır (2018). *Man's Search for Meaning and Religion*, Istanbul: İsyan Publishing.

ce between science (explaining), religion-faith (making sense) and philosophy (both explaining and making sense). Therefore, the way of approaching an event or phenomenon determines whether terms and concepts (reason) or symbols and symbols (imagination) will be used when evaluating it. This choice actually reveals the way of thinking and perspective. After all this explanation, art; It is possible to define it as an activity that is imagination-oriented, intuitive and exists to make sense of what it expresses for its addressee.

Considering that the sacred is the product of the unconscious and intuition (in other words, of imagination, just like art), it is impossible for the sacred not to need indirect expression (signs and symbols) in order to take on a concrete guise. Because, when Paul Tillich talks about God in his work called Systematic Theology (God here can be considered holy), he states that God can never be symbolic because he is an *absolute being*, but depending on man's relationship with him, God can only be seen through symbols. It states that it can be understood-perceivable (Tillich, 1951: 239).

When Tillich's approach to God is accepted within the scope of the sacred phenomenon, in line with this reality; It is inevitable[10] that everything that falls under the heading of the sacred and the sacred from the Ice Age to the present day (God, magic, belief, religion, etc.) has a direct connection and relationship with art.

The fact that the invisible things of God (that is, the ideas and eternal causes of things, through which we know what things should look like/be like) will be seen in the things made, is not only about the things that God makes, but also about the things that are made. The same applies to the things that the bald man himself does. Primitive man cannot have thought of meaning as something

---

10 Jacob Bachofen accepts the *myth* itself as an interpretation of the symbol. According to Bachofen; Anything (things) that the symbol (symbols) try to explain by shaping them as a whole can only be explained by becoming a series of events with myths (myths). For detailed information, see Jacob Bachofen (2019). *Myth, Religion and Matriarchy*, (Trans. Nilgün Şarman), Istanbul: Payel Publishing House, p. 75-77.

that may or may not be added to useful objects at will. Primitive man did not make a distinction between sacred and secular. As a matter of fact, his weapons, clothing, tools and house were all imitations of divine examples, and what they meant to him was more than what they actually were. Here he made them this "excess" (that is, he gave symbolic meanings to his tools) with incantations and rituals... (Coomaraswamy, 2016: 118).

From this perspective, Ice Age artworks can be considered the first symbolic representations of human history.

There are basically two different views about the emergence of symbolic-symbolic understanding and its relationship with society-culture. While some researchers (such as Frazer) argue that there is a tothemic (belief-related) structure at the basis of culture, some scientists (such as Durkheim) argue the opposite; They suggested that social structure and culture create totemism (belief and religion) (Barnard, 2016: 81, 82). Whichever of the two views is accepted, it is seen that a symbolic expression has a direct relationship and bond with belief and social structure. Therefore, it is possible[11] to say that there is a commonality between the indirect narrative style as a form of expression and narrative, and faith (sacred) and art (painting, sculpture, architecture, etc.). Based on this relationship, it would be appropriate to consider art as, in a way, the field of representation (and form of representation) of everything that humans have sanctified since the Ice Age.

---

11   For detailed information about the birth and evolution of symbolic thought, see. Alan Barnard (2016). *The Birth of Symbolic Thought*, (Trans. Mehmet Doğan), Istanbul: Boğaziçi University Publications.

Sky and Divinity

It is possible to see this sacred-art relationship, which started with the first works of art in the Ice Age, in the later period. Göbekli Tepe, dating back to approximately 12,000 years ago, is considered the most important artistic creation of the transition phase between the Ice Age and the Neolithic Period (Mesolithic or Pre-Pottery Neolithic Period) and the beginning of megalithic architecture in a period when there was no organization such as a village yet. However, it is not clear for what purpose Göbekli Tepe, which is a complex of open-topped, circular and spiral spaces consisting of T-shaped obelisks with varying numbers, was built (Photo 2). However, according to both the general opinion of researchers and Klaus Schmidt, who started the archaeological excavations here in 1994, it is extremely likely that Göbekli Tepe (and its successors in the same geography) was built as a place of worship (Schmidt, 2007: 285). Indeed, in a period when there was no settled life yet, Göbekli Tepe was built in a way that did not have a roof, did not meet people's basic needs such as protection and shelter, and gave the impression that it served a ritual or rituals rather than functionality. It is extremely logical to accept it as a whole of temples.

The fact that Göbekli Tepe is considered a temple is also an indication that in the course of the relationship between the sacred and art, the sacred manifests itself in architecture after painting and sculpture.

Göbekli Tepe, which has intense symbolism, still carries a great mystery today with both its architecture and the figurative depictions on its obelisks. Although there is a consensus that the T-shaped stone blocks are a human depiction[12], it is not clear what they symbolically represent (human, God, evil spirits or ancestors) (Schmidt, 2007: 117). Also located on stone blocks; There are many different opinions[13] about animals such as pigs, foxes, snakes, birds, etc. Apart from the interpretations related to these decorations, it is also thought that the B, C and D temple forms in Göbekli Tepe contain a symbolic expression regarding the representation of celestial bodies and body organs in terms of the founding principle of the temple area (Halis, 2016: 55). Some of the prominent views in this context are that Göbekli Tepe was used as an observatory, that it was directly related to the constellations in the sky, or that it showed the scorpion constellation in the Zodiac belt (Bulut, 2018: 21). It is possible to see this sky symbolism, which can be started with Göbekli Tepe, in the belief systems and arts of the civilizations that emerged in the following period. Especially when we look at the pantheons of the first agricultural civilizations such as Mesopotamia and Egypt, the effects of the sky (in this respect, astrology) on belief can be clearly seen (Figure 1)[14].

---

12 *Urfa Man*, a more developed form of this form that can be described as a sculpture, is exhibited in Şanlıurfa Archeology Museum.
13 For a comparative evaluation on this subject, see. Andrew Collins (2017). *Göbekli Tepe The Birth of the Gods*, (Trans. Leyla Tonguç Basmacı), Istanbul: Alfa Publications.
14 In particular, the relationship between astrology, faith and architecture, which cannot be interpreted without focusing on Ptolemy's earth-centered universe model, which remained valid for approximately 1400 years until Copernicus's heliocentric universe theory, is a special subject of study that should be addressed independently. For information about the subject and the relationship between astrology, astronomy and mythology, see. Gülden Bulut (2014). *Mythological Astrology and Psychology*, Izmir: Zodiac Astrology Publications.

In many primitive stone temples, the deity is represented not by a single stone, but by many stones arranged in various styles. (The stone corridors in Britain and the circle formed by the stones in Stonenhenge are the most well-known examples). The arrangements here are not geometric, but seem to have been brought together completely randomly. In reality, this arrangement is an expression of highly developed holiness. (Jung, 2016: 229).

The circle expresses the integrity of the psyche in all its aspects, including the relationship between human and nature integrity. The symbol of the circle, whether in primitive sun worship or modern religion, in myths or dreams, in the mandalas drawn by Tibetan monks, in the land plans of cities or in the global concepts of the first astronomers, always points to the single, most crucial aspect of life, its ultimate unity... (Jung, 2016: 236).

Jung looks at the situation specifically in terms of human psychology and the behavior-practice models that develop accordingly. However, there are also scientists who approach the subject from a metaphysical perspective and have a similar view.

The point transferred in time – a spatial symbol – points to the moment; Psychologically and spiritually speaking, the point is concentration. The circle expresses not only spatial infinity, but also eternity-infinity (that is, temporal infinity). The circle expresses infinity, because it extends the center and reminds us of concentric circles that repeat themselves infinitely. The circle represents eternity because it has neither beginning nor end. The circle reminds us of the roundness of the celestial dome and the horizon and is therefore an image of space... That is why numerical and geometric symbols have their applications not only in space but also in time; These symbols have their applications apriori on ontological, cosmological and spiritual planes, and the cosmic planes are just reflections of these planes. (Schuon, 2016: 91, 92).

What the famous Islamic philosopher Farabi drew attention to regarding the relationship of the *circle* with cosmology is also important in terms of influencing the subsequent process. Farabi states that the sky is the highest among the celestial bodies and divides the sky into nine floors and says that each floor is surrounded by a circular body (Farabi, 2017: 43).

As can be understood from all these interpretations, it is possible to accept the circle form as a geometric symbol of the sky, which humans consider sacred based on the bond they establish with the sky. When Mircea Eliade says that for primitive man, looking at the sky means contacting a transcendent, infinite visibility and experiencing enlightenment (Eliade, 2014: 61), he refers to[15] this quality of the sky (the bond formed between humans).

Based on this existence of the sky and its effect on humans, a sky symbolism that can be started from 10,000-9,000 BC (at the latest) can be mentioned[16]. This symbolic expression, which has gained more importance since humanity's transition to agriculture, has evolved to[17] a completely different dimension, especially with the introduction of the seasons (time cycle) within the sky-time relationship. Being at the closest place to the

---

15 God called out to Moses and Muhammad on the mountain. In a way, the sacred could be heard in a *high place*. Jesus died by being crucified on a hill, close to *the father's* kingdom in the sky.

16 Whether it is associated with the sky itself or the sun, the circle form has become a symbol of perfection and sublimity due to its connection with this sacred. In this context, it is possible to say that the circle was used as a sign of holiness throughout the period of approximately eleven thousand years, from Göbekli Tepe to the temples covered with a central dome. For detailed information about art and circle symbolism, see Saime Tuğrul (2010). *Eternal Sacred Eternal Sacrifice*, Istanbul: İletişim Yayınları, p. 33-90; Dücane Cündi-oğlu (2012). *Architecture and Philosophy*, Istanbul: Kapı Publications, p. 29-36; Ah-met Çaycı (2018). *Meaning and Symbol in Islamic Architecture*, Konya: Palet Publications, p. 61-74. Also, on geometric shapes and symbolism, see. Rene Guenon, (2017). *Symbolism of Horizontal and Vertical Dimensions*, (Trans. Fevzi Topaçoğlu), Istanbul: Human Publications.

17 Mentioned in the relevant paragraph; On evolution related to the sky, seasons, agriculture and belief, see. Muazzez İlmiye Çığ (2011). *Inanna's Love, Faith and Sacred Marriage in Sumer*, Istanbul: Kaynak Publications.

sky, building what is closest to it and trying to bring what is there down to the earth[18] were the most important determinants in the development of the relationship between sacred and art in the following period.

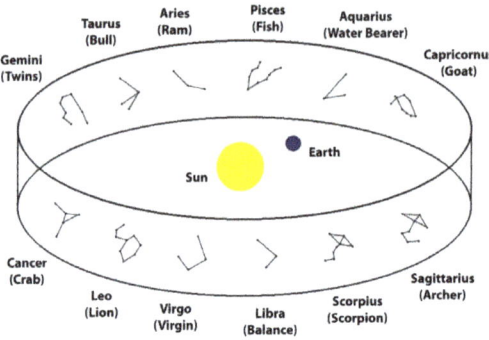

Figure 1: Schematic Drawing of the Sun and Zodiac Constellations.

---

18 Carl Gustav Jung, in his theory called synchronicity versus causality; He states that there may be a simultaneity between flesh and spirit, physics and astrology, and sky and earth. Jung states that this theory can be preferred for things that cannot be explained by the principle of causality, and in summary; In fact, he claims that the sky does not descend to the earth, and that the earth has always existed as its companion. Jung also supports this theory with an experiment he conducted on the relationship between the movements of the planets and married couples (zodiac signs). For detailed information about the experiment and simultaneity theory, see. Carl Gustav Jung (2004). *Simultaneity: A Non-Causal Binding Principle*, (Trans. Levent Özşar), Bursa: Bilos Publications. From this perspective, the action called the effort to bring the sky down to the ground can actually be considered as a structure that must be organized (simultaneously) on the earth.

Photo 2: Göbekli Tepe, Şanlıurfa, 9,000-10,000 BC.

Sky and Anatomy of Human

Regarding the sanctity of the sky, it is necessary to focus on the relationship between the development of human anatomical structure and the sky[19]. Interestingly, in many philosophical and literary texts from the Ancient Period onwards, it is emphasized that there is a relationship between standing upright and competence, selection, difference and awareness. Socrates was one of the first to mention this relationship. Although he did not leave any written work, his student, the Greek historian Xenophon, included the following statement in the fourth chapter of his work containing Socrates' memories:

All walking animals have feet, but the Gods were the first living creatures to make man stand up, so that he could see front and back and look up, so that he would suffer less (Xenophon, 1994: 24).

In addition to this philosophical conclusion of Socrates, many poems were written during the Ancient Greek and Roman periods, emphasizing the special relationship between standing and looking at the sky. Of these, the writings of the famous poet Ovidius (Publius Ovidius Naso), who lived in the 1st century AD, are noteworthy[20].

---

19 Dücane Cündioğlu first mentioned this issue in a video conference. For video conferencing, see Dücane Cündioğlu, *The Origin of Man, Incest and Evolution* (2), https://www.youtu¬be.com/watch?v¬=ykI1_-kcGj-CU&t=3252s. Access Date: 15.04.2020.

20 Although the sanctity of a literary text may seem questionable at first, when the status of poets and people's approach to poetry in the ancient period are considered, it will be seen that these writings should be accepted as the sacred texts of their age.

"No nobility existed yet, no crests,
No not at all, nor was there any honor
Of race; mere beasts and birds of greedy prey,
Together came, because they held the heights,
The arch of stars, the mistress of the world,
The Maker, man, created from divine seed,
In the beginning of the sky, son of Lapetus,
Earth was, in widespread rocks spread wide in the world,
Just earth, heaped up with this vast body's weight;
Earth, felt the thirst of body taken away,
When other animals, by wind and course
Were prone toward the ground, and none of them
Sought a curved flight, but from the turf's smooth mass
Learned to hope for forms of human kind.
He seems to look at nothing but the clouds,
The sky, and seems to hold the stars on high
In lofty places; bitter grace and beauty
He drew into the unknown, changing shape of men."
(Ovidius, 1994: 23).
Translated from Latin (Arthur Golding 1567)

A similar poetic expression is also found in the Islamic inventory. One of the most important texts on Islamic philosophy is Ihvan-ı Safa, written in the 10th century. In the section titled "On the Form of Creation of Animals and Animal Species" in the second volume of the work consisting of four volumes, the feature that distinguishes humans from other living creatures is expressed as follows.

O my brother - may Allah support you and us with a spirit from His presence - know that the images of plants are erected upside down, upside down. Because their heads are towards the center of the earth and their backs are towards the periphery of the heavens. Man is the exact opposite of this. Because wherever he stands on it, in all directions, east, west, south and north, in this or that direction, his head follows the heavens and his feet follow the center of the earth. Animals that do not turn upside down like plants or stand upright like humans are between these two; More precisely, how they turn and dispose in all situations, their heads are towards the horizon and their backs are towards the other horizon opposite it. (İhvan-ı Safa, 2013: 143, 144).

As can be understood from these selected examples, within the ancient teachings of humanity, for thousands of years, it has been tried to emphasize that there is a sacred relationship between the sky and the ability of humans to stand upright and look at it. Starting from the 19th century, after the emergence of modern sciences, human standing upright began to be the subject of biology (based on scientific justifications). Especially in the post-Darwin period, it was emphasized that there was a connection between human intelligence and being able to stand upright, and as a result of the research, being able to stand on two legs changed the structure of the spine and head, this change made the hands usable, and accordingly, human beings started to make various tools. It has been determined that it improves articulate speech (Ünalan, 1997: 114).

As can be seen, it can be claimed that there is a relationship between standing upright and looking at the sky, whether the arguments of faith, philosophy or science have been used from Socrates to the modern age (that is, whether they are mystical or logical in a sense).

Rupert Sheldrake, in his book translated into Turkish as *Someone Watching Me*, gave numerous examples of a person's unconscious awareness that he is being watched, and stated that this ability of modern man to *realize* may have a connection with the lifestyle of the hunter-gatherer period. (Sheldrake, 2004: 225).

If precognitive ability is part of our biological inheritance, fostered by countless generations of natural selection, it is because precognition has a special value. (Sheldrake, 2004: 319).

According to this hypothesis, called *morphogenetic* or *morphic* fields, the *morphic* fields of all species have a history and there is a natural (structural) memory imparted to each species by the process called *morphic resonance* (Sheldrake, 2004: 370). Based on these findings and conclusions[21] of Sheldrake; If we can talk about an ability and structural change that has evolved through tens of thousands of years of struggle for survival, we can also talk about behaviors-abilities and even changing-developing physical characteristics that are the product of tens of thousands of years of effort to become a society and survive as a society.

---

21 For another work of the author related to the subject, see: Rupert Sheldrake (2001). *A New Science of Life*, (Trans. Sezer Soner), İzmir: Ege-Meta Publications.

Examples of Phenomenon

Ancient India, together with Mesopotamia, constitutes one of the most important basins in the history of faith. In Hinduism, which has many different renewal processes, with the end of the Vedic period, a triple God concept consisting of Brahma (creator), Vishnu (preserver) and Shiva (destroyer) was established (Bose, 2016: 103). It is believed that Vishnu, one of these three Gods, protects the disrupted order and balance by descending to the world through his avatars (incarnations) at various periods[22] (Photo 3). The last six of the ten generally accepted avatars of Vishnu to date have manifested into the world in human form[23] (Gül, 2018: 452). The most remarkable and important of these last six avatars[24] is Siddhartha Gotama Budda, who is believed to have been born as the ninth avatar of Vishnu and will later be accepted as the founder of Buddhism. It is accepted that she became pregnant innocently by an elephant entering her body

---

22 According to Louis Renou, manifestation through avatars passed from Vishnu to Shiva and was subsequently used to deify many heroes in Indian history. For detailed information, see Louis Renou (2016). *Hinduism*, (Trans. Maide Selen), Istanbul: İletişim Publishing, p. 44-49.
23 According to Hinduism, it is still believed that Vishnu will return to earth with its eleventh avatar.
24 Mohiniattam Dance, one of the classical and ancient Indian dances, takes its name from Mohini, one of Vishnu's avatars, who prevents the destruction of the universe by dancing. For Mohiniattam and other Indian dances, see Rukiye Bilican (2017). *Religious Basis of Indian Dances*, Master's Thesis, Marmara University Social Sciences Institute, Ankara.

from her right side [25](Photo 4) (Eliade, 2019: 96). In Indian Mythology, Vishnu's name when he falls asleep is called Narayana. One day, when Narayana fell asleep and woke up, he took out a lotus flower containing Brahma from his navel and created the one who created it (Pattanaik, 2006: 57). As can be seen from this example, various themes that show similarities with the self-pregnancy and birth of Buddha's mother are also present in Hinduism, the religion from which Buddhism emerged.

It is possible to see something similar to the sacred manifestation events in India in the geography of Iran. According to Iranian Mythology, three great saviors from the descendants of Zoroaster will emerge in the last three thousand years of the world (Yıldırım, 2012: 518, 519). The common feature of these three saviors, named Oşider (Hoşider), Oşidermah (Huşidermah) and Soshyant, is that they were and will be[26] born from a virgin young girl[27]. In some stories about Soshyant, the last savior, it is also mentioned that the savior-hero will be given birth by a virgin woman who got pregnant from Zarathustra in an otherworldly way (Leeming, 2001: 149). The most important feature of the Soshyant, apart from its occurrence as a sacred manifestation, is that it is responsible for the work of arranging and correcting the world[28].

---

25 In some sources, it is accepted that he entered his mother's womb as himself, not an elephant. See Bhikkhu Nanamoli (2001). *The Life of Buddha*, Onalaska (USA): BPE Press, p. 2-4.
26 According to Zoroastrian belief, the first two saviors were born.
27 It is believed that three virgins will become pregnant and give birth to these heroes from the sperm that Zarathustra left in Lake Hâmûn (Yıldırım, 2008: 400). A similar motif exists in Hinduism. According to Indian Mythology, when Shiva and Parvati's lovemaking was interrupted, Shiva's semen flowed into the Ganges River and impregnated the wives of the six wise men who were bathing there at that moment. Later, the fetuses unite and a six-headed warrior hero is formed. (Pattanaik, 2006: 194).
28 This savior understanding also has a relationship with the Mahdi-Messiah belief seen in different cultures and religions. For detailed information, see Ömer Faruk Harman (2017). "The Pre-Islamic Background of the Expected Savior Belief", Expected Savior Belief, Istanbul: KURAMER Publications, p. 41-59

A narrative describing the birth of the Mongol ruler Genghis Khan is similar to the Indian and Iranian examples. According to legend, Genghis Khan's mother became pregnant with Genghis Khan as a result of a luminous tail entering the tent through the chimney hole and seeping into her body (Eliade, 2016: 154). According to the Sumerian belief system, it is possible to see a rich sexual symbolism in Sumerian Mythology, since the source of prosperity on earth and the happiness of people is the sexual intercourse between the gods (Kramer, 2002: 364). Within this rich inventory, the myth telling the love story of Goddess Inanna and God Dumuzi is of great importance not only for Sumer but also for the entire Mesopotamian belief tradition. The myth generally deals with Goddess Inanna choosing God Dumuzi to marry, Inanna going underground after the marriage, and the reunion of the couple after being separated for a while[29] (Altuncu, 2014: 157,158). The marriage ceremony that takes place in this myth, which is the symbolic expression of a seasonal cycle within the concept of abundance and prosperity, was later transformed into a ritual by the Sumerian kings and their successors[30]. From many written sources and descriptions on cylinder seals, it is seen that Sumerian kings and priestesses representing Inan-

---

29 The goddess of beauty and sky, who first appeared as Inanna, would later evolve into Ishtar, As-tarte and Aphrodite in the Mesopotamia-Cyprus-Greek Peninsula triangle.
30 Marija Gimbutas traces the origin of the regenerative goddess figure in this sacred marriage related to a seasonal cycle back to the Ice Age. Gimbutas, who accepts the earth as feminine, establishes a relationship between femininity and the renewal activity on earth, which began to be seen since the Ice Age; He emphasizes that some female figurines with prominent limbs are linked to this relationship (Photo 5). At the same time, the author states that birth-occurrence is cosmically related to the goddess cult, and interprets the tombs and tomb architecture symbolically as the wombs of the feminine earth. For detailed information, see Marija Gimbutas (2001). *The Living Goddesses*, California: University of California Press.

na performed this sacred ritual by having sexual intercourse[31] (Campbell, 2016: 51,52).

Princesses, wives of city lords and kings, carried out the administrative affairs of the temple as high priestesses of the male gods. One of their important duties was to replace Goddess Inanna in sacred marriage ceremonies and marry the king who represented God Dumuzi…

A special duty of the priestesses in the temples, especially in the temples of Inanna, was general femininity, a kind of prostitution. They were considered sacred because they served God… (Çığ, 2019: 78).

This ritual found a response not only from the kings but also from the subjects in later periods. The noteworthy point here is; Over time, a sacred institution of prostitution, supported by various festivals[32], emerged in a wide geography from West Africa to Anatolia, from Mesopotamia to India, and if pregnancy occurred as a result of this union, the children were considered to belong to God. For example, dancer girls serving in Tamil temples in India were called deva-dasis (servants of God), but they were referred to as prostitutes among the public (Frazer, 2018: 75). On the Slave Coast of West Africa, women working in temples were also found among the Ewe-speaking peoples. The main occupation of these women was prostitution, and in each town, the most beautiful girls between the ages of ten and twelve were accepted into the temple. Girls would stay in these temples for

---

31   In the Mesopotamian belief system, kings not only represented God (in special rituals), but were also accepted as God themselves. In the case of Mesopotamia, this tradition changed with the Babylonian ruler Hammurabi. For the Hammurabi Period and the changes in the state structure, see. Horst Klengel (2019). *King Hammurabi and the Babylonian Diary*, (Trans. Nesri Oral), Ankara: Totem Publications.

32   For detailed information about Sacred Prostitution and festivals related to this ritual, see. James George Frazer (1917). *The Golden Bough A Study In Magic And Religion (Part I The Magic Art Evolution Of Kings)*, C: 2, London: Macmillan and Co. Limited Press, p. 128-138.

three years, learn to sing and dance, act as prostitutes to priests and students of priest schools, and then become general prostitutes. It was assumed that these women married God, and the children born from such unions were considered to belong to God (Frazer, 2018: 80).

In the Mesopotamian tradition, the most important and well-known figure that can be evaluated within the phenomenon of no-father birth is undoubtedly Jesus. Although not verbatim[33], it is stated in both the Bible and the Quran that Jesus was born fatherless from the virgin Mary[34].

In the sixth month of Elizabeth's pregnancy, God sent the Angel Gabriel to the city of Nazareth in Galilee to the girl engaged to a man named Joseph, a descendant of David. The girl's name was Mariam. The angel came to her and said, "Greetings, O maiden who has attained the grace of God! "The Lord is with you," he said. Meryem, who was very surprised by what was said, started to think about what this greeting could mean. But the angel said to her, "Do not be afraid, Mary; you have found favor with God. Behold, you will conceive and give birth to a son, and you

---

33 Although there are sectarian differences, Jesus is accepted as the son of God by Christians, but according to Islamic belief, he is not the son of God but his prophet. For detailed information on this subject, see: Zekiye Sönmez (2002). *"The Prophet in the Light of the Bible and the Quran. Jesus", III. Proceedings of the History of Religions Research Symposium (9-10 June 2001)*, Ankara: History of Religions Association Publications, p. 137-166.

34 In this section, Jesus is evaluated as the subject of mythology (science), not religion (belief), and is treated as a socio-cultural figure, not a religious one. For Christians or Muslims, even mentioning the name of Jesus in such an article can be seen as extremely objectionable and wrong. However, when it is considered that all the phenomena (and/or rituals) discussed mythologically in the book today are the very requirements of faith and belief in the age in which they occurred or were believed in, it will be seen that the examples are ontologically no different from each other. There are also groundbreaking studies about Jesus, not as a religious figure but as a historical figure. For such a study, see. Ay-tunç Altındal (2018). *Which Jesus is Apollonius of Tyana*, Istanbul: Destek Publications.

will call his name Jesus. He will be great and will be called 'Son of the Most High'. The Lord God will give him the throne of his ancestor David. And he will reign over the Lineage of Jacob forever, and his dominion will have no end." Mary asked the angel, "How can this happen? "I didn't reach manhood," he said. The angel answered him: "The Holy Spirit will come upon you, and the power of the Most High will overshadow you. Therefore the one to be born will be called holy, the Son of God. Look, Elizabeth, one of your relatives, also conceived a son in her old age. This woman, known to be barren, is now in her sixth month. There is nothing God cannot do." "I am the servant of the Lord," said Mary. "Let it be done as you say." After that the angel left him. (Luke, 1/28-35).

When the angels said: "O Mary! Allah gives you the good news of a word from Himself that his name is Jesus Christ, son of Mary. He is respected in this world and the hereafter and is one of those who are very close to Allah." He will speak to people both in the cradle and in adulthood, and he will be among the righteous." (Mary) said, "O my Lord! She said, "How can I have a child when no human being has touched me?" Allah said, "Yes, but Allah creates whatever He wishes. "When He wishes something to happen, He just says to it, 'Be', and it is." (Quran: Al-i Imran 45-47).

The pregnancy of Mary and the birth of Jesus, which follow a course parallel to the sacred birth rituals originating from Mesopotamia, are the last and most important example that can be mentioned within the tradition of no-father birth in Mesopotamia, as a subject not of religion but of mythology (science)[35] (Photo 6).

---

35 Joseph Campbell claims that since Luke was Greek, this birth story in the Gospel of Luke originates from Greek Mythology. See Campbell, Joseph and Moyers, Bill (2007). *The Power of Mythology, Mythology and Stories from Holy Books to Hollywood Movies*, (Trans. Zeynep Yaman), Istanbul: MediaCat Books, p. 224.

Since Jesus was Jewish, it is necessary to briefly mention the place of the phenomenon in Jewish belief (within the Mesopotamian belief tradition). Although there were no sacred births similar to Jesus or other examples in the Jewish society before Christ, women impregnated by God (Lord) are mentioned several times in various parts of the Tanakh.

The angel of the LORD appeared to the woman and said, "Although you are barren and childless, you will become pregnant and give birth to a son." (Tanakh: Judges, 13/3).

He makes the barren woman stay at home and makes her a happy mother with children. Praise the LORD! (Tanakh: Psalms, 113/9).

O barren woman who bears no children, shout for joy; O you, who don't know what birth pain is, shout and shout with joy. For the abandoned woman will have more children than the married woman," says the Lord (Tanakh: Isaiah, 54/1).

This *familiarity* of Judaism with the phenomenon of no-father birth (the miracle of faith) is one of the most important reasons why Jesus was not considered strange in the society of that period because he was born without a father[36].

The image of the sky and the sun in Egyptian Mythology is so important that it has been influential and guiding not only in the belief system, but also in a wide range of areas, from architecture to dynasty structure, from social life to the kingship system. So much so that, in addition to the pyramids of the Old Kingdom period being structures built based on celestial symbolism, Pharaohs in the Egyptian belief system were directly identified with God Ra (Strano, 2018: 455).

---

36 I would like to point out that the determination made here is a completely personal interpretation. Because all of the canonical Bibles were written between 70-150 AD. Therefore, the earliest of the Gospels (whether canonical or apocryphal) in which Mary's pregnancy with Jesus is described dates from approximately 40 years after the death of Jesus.

Since social order represents one aspect of the cosmic order, kingship must have existed from the beginning of the world. The Creator had become the first king; He handed over this task to his son and successor, Pharaoh. As a matter of fact, the gestures of the Pharaoh are described in terms used to describe God Ra or his sacred manifestations[37]. (Eliade, 2018a: 130).

Based on these explanations, it is possible to accept everyone who became a pharaoh as a manifestation-son of God, depending on the sanctity of the pharaonic position. Erik Hornoung also states that in the historical process, in Egypt, God was first manifested as inanimate objects, then as plants and animals, and finally as humans, and that, especially during the old kingdom period, the pharaohs were considered the sons of the Sun God who created the world. (Hornoung, 2014: 77, 99).

Dionysus[38] is the ancient god of wine, relationship, entertainment and ecstasy (Grimal, 2012: 153). But apart from what he represents, Dionysus is actually an important figure[39] that needs to be considered in a much broader context. The most important feature that makes Dionysus different from other gods and goddesses in the Greek Pantheon is that his mother is Semele, a mortal virgin[40]

---

37 The pyramids were called m(e)r, which means Ascension in Egyptian, and the pharaohs were actually greeting the sun god Ra through these huge mausoleums (Roth, 2002: 241).

38 Bacchus as it is known in Rome.

39 It is possible to interpret Dionysus within the scope of the life-cosmic world tree phenomenon by associating it with the cult of Dumuzi, Tammuz, Adonis and Hızır. For detailed information about the mentioned topics, see. Joseph Campbell (2015). *Western Mythology Masks of God*, (Trans. Kudret Emi-roğlu), Istanbul: Islık Publications, p. 14-49; Ahmet Yaşar Ocak (2012). *Hızır or Hızır İlyas Cult in Turkish Islamic Beliefs*, Istanbul: Kabalcı Publications, p. 145-162.

40 Dionysus, who was first born to Semele, was later born a second time by his father Zeus. For the birth and life of Dionysus, see. Mareel Detienne, (2010). *"Dionysos Matter"*, Dictionary of Mythologies, (Trans. Nusat Çoka), (Dir. Yves Bonnefoy, Turkish Publication Editor. Levent Yılmaz), C: 1, Ankara: Dost Kitabevi Yayınları, p. 172-179.

(Akgezer, 2018: 26, 27). Dionysus, who symbolized joy and fun even though he had a very painful birth and life[41], can also be considered the most secular god of the ancient world, due to having an earthly mother, even though his father was a divine figure (Photo 7). Considering that the reenactments in the parades held in the name of Dionysus, which turned into a ritual, turned into tragedy and comedy over time (Grimal, 2012: 155) and led to the birth of theater and then (indirectly) of all performing arts, the traces of this worldliness[42] have continued until today. It can be said that it extends. In this respect, theaters, in addition to being temples built in the name of Dionysus, are also examples of the concretization of the abstract sacred in the eyes of society through architecture (Photo 8)[43].

---

41 In fact, although they seem opposite, pain and fun are very related to each other. The following lines of the Lesbosian poet Alcaeus, who lived in the 6th century BC, shed light on this relationship: Let's drink! Why should we wait for the lamps? Daylight is already a finger away. O beloved, bring forth the great ornate cups! The son of Seme-le and Zeus gave wine to people to ease their pain. (Quoted by: Akurgal, 2005: 325).
42 Dionysus, who is essentially a plant-tree god and is represented by animals such as ox, capricorn and goat, is one of the most important festivals in many agriculture-harvest-product focused festivals, especially in the Anatolian rural geography today, in parallel with the Dumuzi-Adonis-Osiris-Attis cults. It is one of the archetypes in its origin. For detailed information, see James George Frazer (2016). *Golden Branch The Origins of Religion and Folklore*, (Translated by Mehmet H. Doğan), Istanbul: Yapı Kredi Publications, p. 154-240.
43 Dionysus as a god also existed in the pre-Ancient Greek period, during the Mycenaean Civilization (1,450-1,100 BC) (Armstrong, 2019: 48). This situation is important as it shows the emergence of the Dionysus figure and its relationship with Mesopotamian cultures-beliefs.

Photo 3: Depiction of Vishnu, 10-11 AD. Century, Metropolitan Museum of Art, (https://www.metmuseum.org/).

Photo 4: Conception and Birth of Buddha, Architectural Plastic, 5-6. Century, Metropolitan Museum of Art, (https://www.metmuseum.org/).

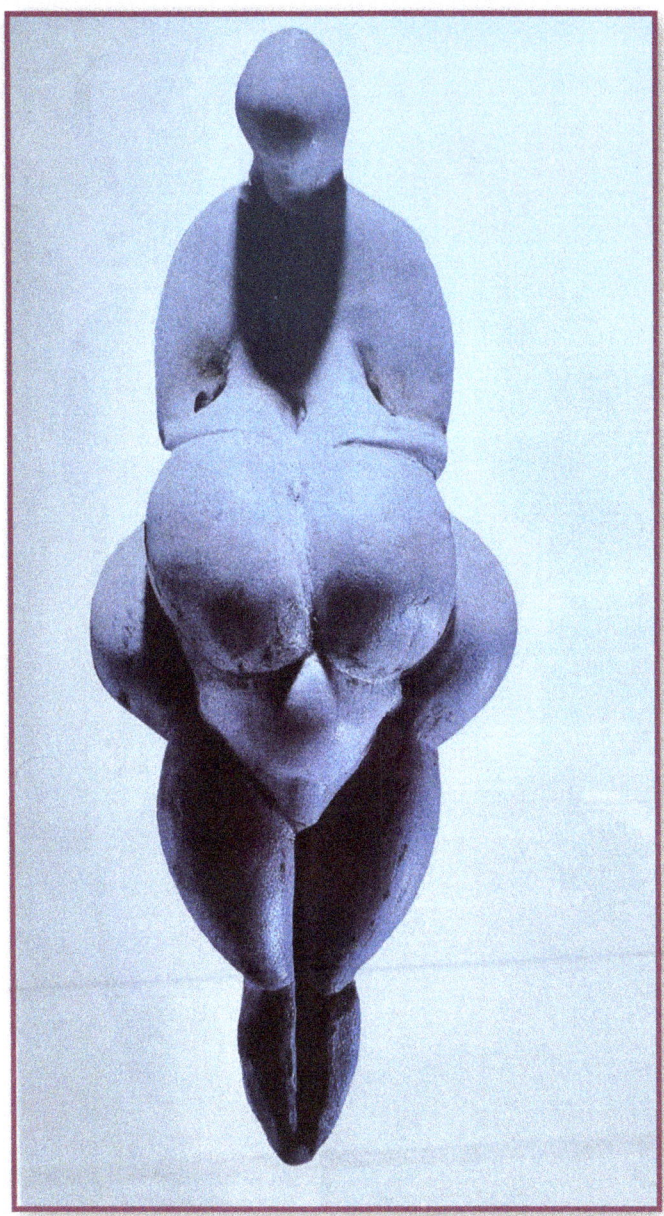

Photo 5: Female Figurine, 23,000 BC, (Marija Gimbutas).

Photograph 6: Prostration of Magi to Jesus, Hieronymus Bosch, 1475. Metropolitan Museum of Art, (https://www.metmuseum.org/).

Photo 7: Allegory of Bacchus and Autumn, Filippo Parodi 1630-1702, Metropolitan Museum of Art, (https://www.metmuseum.org/).

Photo 8: Ephesus Ancient City Theatre, 1-2 AC. Century, Selçuk/İzmir

Religion, State and Power

In all the examples discussed in the previous section, it can be seen that all those born without fathers, who are essentially a manifestation of the sacred, are somehow related to the sky, albeit in different ways[44]. This relationship, as tried to be expressed in the relevant sections of the text, is directly related to the idea of being close to the sky and bringing the sky down to the ground.

...As in Denys's "celestial hierarchy" painting, God's reign reigns over everything, but the executor of this reign is not himself but his angels; This celestial hierarchy defines sacred power rather than a sacred order; Angels are like ministers of God. According to Denys' basic idea, what is ordered within the hierarchy is the sacred and divine. (Quoted by: Tuğrul, 2014: 76).

---

44 Joseph Campbell calls this phenomenon virgin birth. Campbell states that the creative spirit of the father is realized (manifested) through an intermediary called the mother of the world, and that the primordial sea in many different cultures is actually related to being born from a virgin, and that the female figure being a virgin is related to her being pregnant from the invisible unknown (Campbell , 2019: 263). One of Campbell's examples to support this theory is interesting. According to the narrative in Finnish Mythology; The virgin daughter of the air left her home in the sky to swim in the endless waters, and after swimming for seven hundred years, she became pregnant and first created the sky, the sun, the moon and the clouds, and then shaped the world. For detailed information, see Joseph Campbell (2019). *The Hero's Infinite Journey*, (Trans. Sabri Gürses), Istanbul: İthaki Publications, p. 263-279.

Especially the laying of the foundation[45] of the state in the 4,000s BC and the institutionalization of this phenomenon in Mesopotamia in the 3,000s BC enabled the phenomenon of no-father birth to develop in the power-legitimacy-reign trilogy. When we look at the examples mentioned and not mentioned in the book as a whole, it is seen that in all manifestations (occurrence-becoming), an authority arises in the hands of the one who is created (born or created). The fact that the holders of this authority (if they are not manifested as God himself) are mostly administrators (king-ruler) and the other part are a founder-defender of religion or a hero, in legal terms, the authority is in two centers of power (which will unite over time); It shows that religion and state are centralized. In this context, it is inevitable that the figure[46], which comes into being as a manifestation of the most sacred, also carries a divine authority[47].

---

45 Regarding the birth of the state, see. Marcela Frangipane (2002). *The Birth of the State in the Near East*, (Trans. Z. Zühre İlkgelen), Istanbul: Arkeoloji Sanat Publications.

46 Erhan Altunay states that one of the most important archetypes for men is the king (ruler) and for the man of the pagan society; It states that the responsibilities-duties carried by the king as the image of God on earth and the responsibilities-duties carried by the man within the family institution are perceived as the same. This determination is extremely important as it shows the dimensions in which the relationship between the phenomenon of the sacred and the phenomenon of being born without a father can evolve and be reduced. For detailed information, see Erhan Altunay (2014). *Paganizm-I Introduction to Ancient Wisdom*, Istanbul: Hermes Publications, p. 214-225

47 Alaeddin Şenel developed an interesting approach model to this issue and interpreted this transformation in the god-human relationship as not the deification of man, but the humanization of God. For detailed information, see Alaeddin Şenel (2019). History of Humanity, Istanbul: İmge Kitabevi, p. 406-408. This situation is also related to the theory of symbolism defended by Durkheim, expressed in footnote 8. For detailed information about Durkheim's theory of religion, which he argued emerged as a product of society, see. Emile Durkheim (2005). *Primitive Forms of Religious Life*, (Trans. Fuat Aydın), Istanbul: Ataç Publications.

In order for the political system to maintain its existence, it needs legitimacy and legitimizing support. It is difficult for the state to exercise its authority and power without legitimacy and support. This legitimacy and support is provided by the political system through various means, such as an institution, organization, or group, legitimacy such as tradition, belief, religion, law, ideology, a rational justification, charisma, a cultural element. (Okumuş, 2005: 42).

As Ejder Okumuş stated, the existence and sustainability of the state depends on various legitimizers. In this respect, it seems that the most ancient legitimizing power is religion, which is the institutionalized form of belief[48]. Depending on this legitimizing power of religion; In the historical process, the fact that rulers are seen as characters full of power and that kings-rulers in different cultures[49] are considered (similarly) as the incarnation of the creator, as human-God and as representatives of God (Sarıkçı-oğlu,

---

48 Alexander the Great, known by names such as İskender-i Kebir, İskender-i Zülkarneyn, is also an extremely important figure in terms of Persian Mythology. II. The belief that Alexander the Great, the son of Philip, was a descendant of Herakles (Hercules), a mythological (religious) figure and demi-God (Yıldırım, 2008: 427), is a requirement of this authoritarian understanding (Photo 9). A similar understanding of legitimation is also seen in Asian societies. In a letter he wrote to the King of France, Mangu Khan said; It is stated that the only eternal God in the sky and his only master on earth is his son, Genghis Khan (Harva, 2014: 111). Although it is not called the son of God, a similar understanding is also seen in Asian Turks. According to the Gokturk Inscriptions, the reign of Bilge Khagan was realized by God's choice and will (initiative). See Muharrem Ergin (2003). *Göktürk Books*, Istanbul: Boğaziçi Publications, p. 7, 19, 33.

49 In the Sassanids, one of the ancient states of Iran, rulers were accepted as manifestations of God and brothers of the sun and the moon (Yıldırım, 2008: 525). A similar understanding is also seen in Northern European cultures within the understanding of sacred marriage. For detailed information, see Gro Steinsland (2015). *"Rulers as Children of Gods and Giant Women: On the Mythology of Pagan Northern Rulers", Viking World*, (Ed. Stefan Brink and Neil Priece), (Trans. Ebru Kılıç), Istanbul: Alfa Publications, p. 281-289.

2011: 190) gains an explanation. In this context, the phenomenon of no-father birth is a means of coexistence and existence that humans create at the end of the process of becoming a society, in other words; It is possible to justify (and relate)[50] it to the existence of the social (superior) mind, that is, the state[51]. The product of the superior mind emphasized here is the contract, which, according to many political philosophers, is the fundamental basis of the state. This contract, which can be defined as the rule of law (constitution) in today's world, constitutes the main reference that gives power. Therefore, the fact that this contract, which enables power

---

50 This justification is also parallel to the unifying and integrative nature of religion. According to sociologist Peter L. Berger's theory of sociology of religion, religion; It serves the mission of sanctifying and legalizing human-centered social rules and institutions by giving a cosmic reference (Berger, 2015: 95).

51 Apart from Northern Europe, it would be appropriate to give an example from the Far East on the subject: According to Japanese Mythology, a divine lineage began to pass on to mortals with the descent of the Heavenly Descendant Ninigi-no-mikoto to the earth and his marriage. Depending on this marriage myth, all subsequent Japanese emperors had a divine lineage, and this created the phenomenon of divine sovereignty. On the subject, see. Michael Ashkenazi (2003). Japanese Mythology, (Trans. Özlem Özarpacı), Istanbul: Say Publications, p. 260,261-326,327. This understanding was not limited to the Japanese belief system; the Japanese emperor was accepted as a sacred figure in the first Japanese Constitution dated 1899. For detailed information, see Merve Balcıoğlu (2018). *"Public Administration in Japan and the Unique Aspects of Japanese Political Culture"*, Turkish Studies, C: 11, P: 56, p. 709-719. The traces of this acceptance, both in belief and in the legal system, can be seen in Japan in the Second World War. It is possible to see it until World War II. Emperor Hiroito, who was the Japanese Emperor in World War II and was considered a divine figure, destroyed many traditions and historical missions of Japanese emperors for the first time after the war was lost (Photo 10). The concept of the emperor-king, embodied as the son of the sky, is not limited to Japan in the Far East. In ancient Chinese religion, emperors were directly named as the sons of the sky, and even the troubles experienced by the state were attributed to not complying with the movements and functioning of the sky. For detailed information, see Annamaria Schimmel (1999). *Introduction to the History of Religions*, Istanbul: Kırkambar Publications, p. 24-26.

to rule and obliges people to obey (almost from its first appearance until the modern age), is related to sacred-divine references is extremely normal[52] for the times when the perception of religion and state was dominant in society. Thomas Hobbes explains the power of divine authority against worldly authority as follows:

...if another authority appears in front of the sovereign and tries to limit or even dominate him, claiming that he gets his power from God, it will fall apart like a castle made of playing cards. (Quoted by: Ağaoğulları and Köker, 2018: 247).

The sound of ascension, which is seen in many different cultures and religions as the transfer of authority from the sky to the earth, is an important theme that should be mentioned within the phenomenon of no-father birth. Although there are different types, the act of ascending to heaven is an activity of ascending to heaven and coming back[53], whether spiritual or physical. In many examples, the figure who is a king or who will later become a king rises to the sky, meets with God or gods, and returns to earth[54] by taking something that will give him authority (sometimes this can be an object). This incident is very important as it is the way in which a divine authority is obtained. So much so that, from Mesopotamia to Egypt, from Anatolia to the Greek Peninsula, it is possible to see many king figures who ascended to the sky, contacted God (gods) and were given the right to rule.

---

52 For detailed information about the share of divine authority in the establishment of the state, the contract and the relations between the ruler and the ruled, see. Mehmet Ali Akoğulları and Levent Köker (2018). *King-State or Mortal God*, Istanbul: İmge Kitabevi; Mehmet Ali Akoğulları and Levent Köker (2017). *From Empire to the State of God*, Istanbul: İmge Kitabevi.

53 Miraj, in which the Islamic prophet Muhammad lived, is an ascension to the sky and return, and the word miraculous, derived from the verb arece, means staircase. For the miraculous event mentioned in the Holy Quran, see. *Surah Al-Isra 17/1* and *Surah An-Najm 53/13-18*

54 For detailed information about the Ascension Theme, its types, the tools used and the objects obtained, see. Şinasi Gündüz, Yavuz Ünal and Ekrem Sandıkçıoğlu (1996). *Ascension Motifs in Religions*, Ankara: Vadi Publications.

This theme, seen specifically in the king figure in many different states in the Mesopotamian tradition, began to be seen within the institution of prophethood in the post-Judaic period[55].

Whether or not it used ascending to heaven and coming back as a tool, the attempt to bring down this authority, based in Mesopotamia, from the sky to the earth experienced a change and development with the politicization of Judaism and the rule of Solomon[56]. By the 10th century BC, the understanding that God (the holy) was manifested on earth with the state as the owner of absolute power, that the temple built in the name of God was the objective counterpart of the sacred relationship between God-state-people, and that the temple should be built as a symbol of power on earth began to be seen in monotheist religions[57]. From this perspective, it can be said that Solomon's form of power and his understanding of the temple directly or indirectly influenced the monotheist religions of the later period, especially the various understandings and practices of Islam[58].

In Shia thought, which represents the more esoteric[59] side of Islam compared to the Sunni school; Depending on the fact that what belongs to God (the sacred) is manifested in man (or prophet) with a naming such as *Sainthood or the seal of prophethood*,

---

55 The fact that both Moses and later Muhammad were born as orphans is actually related to the image of the orphan hero, and this can be interpreted as a type of the phenomenon of being born without a father or as an extension of the change he went through.

56 According to Judaism and Christianity, he is a king, and according to Islam, he is a prophet. For detailed information, see. Ömer Faruk Harman (2010). "*The Article of Solomon*", TDV Encyclopedia of Islam, Ankara: TDV Publications, C: 38, p. 60-62.

57 The only difference between the monotheist approach and the previous period is; The reason is that the power and authority on earth belongs to a superior chosen one, not to a figure who is the son of God (the holy).

58 For a specific study on the traces of this interaction in the shrine-temple context, see. Stefanos Yerasimos (2014). Constantinople and Hagia Sophia Legends in Turkish Texts, Istanbul: İletişim Publications.

59 The word Esoteric is used as an adjective here.

and this *Sainthood* can be transferred through blood, it is believed that God (Allah) is manifested in man and according to that, there are various thoughts about the emergence of an authority in the person who is manifested accordingly[60]. Moreover, within the polarity in Islam, that is, the idea of gathering God's will in a human center; It is also worth noting that there is an understanding of the *most qualified human* being in Islam, who can be considered not directly of God (Allah) himself but as his servant and, in a sense, his most distinguished creation[61].

What the divine names and attributes are concerned with, not in the divine essence itself, but in the primordial manifestation, in the "fourteen innocent levels" (the Prophet, Fatima and the twelve imams), as the hadith states, is this "anthropomorphic" form appropriate to the essence of God which they are the basis of nouns and adjectives in the Qur'an...

... Sainthood is the title worthy of God's friend, loved one, God's friend and lover. This divine closeness is the source of the prophetic duty in the Prophet himself.; It is the inwardness that he did not reveal as the prophet who brought sharia. This revelation of the West is the Imam's fascination with absolute Sainthood from the Prophet. Just as it is the prophet's seal of prophethood through which God sealed his prophethood, it is also the seal of I.Imam's absolute Sainthood. (Corbin, 2016: 211, 212).

Although the transfer is not required to be through blood ties[62], it is possible to see the manifestation of the sacred in hu-

---

60 See *Ghulat-i Şi'a or Galiyye*.
61 It is possible to relate and establish a similarity between this concept of the Perfect Man, which is dominant in Islamic thought, and the concept of Elohim Hayim in Jewish mysticism. In addition, in the mystical Jewish teaching Kabbalah, there is the concept of messiah, which is the image of a distinguished person in whom the names of God are manifested. For detailed information, see İzzet Erş (2019). *Interpretation of the Sacred, Hermeneutic Essays on Sacred Texts*, Istanbul: Siyah Kitap Publications, p. 101-177; 362-364.
62 Seyyidness, Sheriffness, see. Mustafa Sabri Küçükaşçı (2009). *"Seyyid Article"*, TDV Islam Encyclopedia, Ankara: TDV Publications, C: 37, p. 40-43.

mans as a transfer of authority-custody in the rest of the Islamic world. The fact that manifestation in Islamic thought is in the dimension of custody-authority and that figures that are the sons of God are not seen is directly related to the understanding and interpretation of unity in Islamic thought.

The refusal to identify any concrete form, even symbolically, with God, the absence of an icon that could symbolize the God-man or incarnation found in other traditions, stems from the Islamic insistence on Divine unity. Since there is no sacred image in Islam as in Christianity, man cannot somehow design himself by identifying with the god-man image (Nasr, 2017: 239, 240).

In parallel with the thought that Seyyed Hossein Nasr tried to summarize, it makes sense why those in authority who were born as the son of God are not seen in the Islamic World[63], but in fact the phenomenon continues to exist by changing its identity and the understanding of the son of God (indirectly), seems that it is continued[64] with titles[65] such as God's whip, God's shadow and God's sword.

---

63 In fact, it is not correct to explain this change only with the practices of Islamic belief and thought, but it also has a direct relationship with the changing world-state perception and the conditions of the age, especially in the post-Roman Empire period. An example of this is that in the medieval Western world, the Pope maintained his presence as the spiritual representative of Jesus and also represented a political authority.

64 The first practice that can be called the prototype of the idea of centralizing and gathering divine authority in a polytheistic world is seen in the Jews. Among the Israelites, who were in a polytheistic pattern, Prophet Elijah was the first to state that only their local god, Yahweh, should be worshiped. Within this belief system, which includes a god specific to a race, the institution of prophecy seems to be limited to the royal palaces of Israel and Judah (Armstrong, 2019: 99).

65 For detailed information about other titles used in Islamic States, see. Abdülkerim Özaydın (2012). "Title Clause", TDV Islamic Encyclopedia, C: 42, p. 163-166; Mehmet İpşirli (2012). "Title Article Ottomans", TDV Islamic Encyclopedia, C: 42, p.166; Ahmet Çaycı (2019). *Planet and Zodiac Sign Depictions in Anatolian Seljuk Art,* Konya: Palet Publications

Şinasi Gündüz makes the following determination in his work Between Mythology and Faith:
Is it right to confine myths only to past periods and primitive cultures and exclude today's people from this? Are myths only a legacy of ancient cultures that were fictionalized in the past and have been passed down from generation to generation until today? Are there not current examples of origin myths, future myths, hero myths and similar myths produced by modern people? In fact, when the individual and social structure, feelings and thoughts, hobbies, phobias, desires and demands of today's people are examined, it is understood that myths do not only belong to the primitive cultures of the past period, but today's people also produce many myths of almost all kinds and keep them alive. (Gündüz, 1998: 29, 30).

In parallel with these findings, Gündüz also said; He states that there is a similarity between the ancient people's search for a hero-superior person and the desire of Muslims to trace their lineage to various religious elders, especially the Islamic prophet Muhammad (Gündüz, 1998: 30, 31).

The fact that the power-state-reign needs a sacred reference to legitimize its power is also related to the fact that this reference has a counterpart in human beings. To see an emperor as the son of God in the mid-twentieth century was also, in a sense, to want to see. Likewise, in the more recent past and today, believing in people with religious discourse was also about wanting to believe in that person and feeling the need to believe. This state of believing-wanting to believe is related to the hero image (partially emphasized in the fifty-fifth footnote), which is indirectly related[66] to the phenomenon described in the book as no-father birth.

---

[66] The hero that is valid for everyone and is the easiest to find is the ancestor. The tradition of giving children the names of their grandfathers is a method used to immortalize the deceased ancestor in line with this idea. For a study on the subject specifically for the Middle East, see. Pierre Bou-dieu (2019). *Eril Tahakkum*, (Trans. Bediz Yılmaz), Istanbul: Akşam Publications, p. 25-36.

Photo 9: Bust of Alexander the Great, Viktor Brodzki, 19th Century, Metropolitan Art Museum, (https://www.metmuseum.org/).

Photo 10: Mausoleum of Japanese Emperor Hiroito, Kyoto / Japan, (Bridgecross, https://en.wikipedia.org/).

The Phenomenon of No-Father Birth and Architecture

The effects of the phenomenon of no-father birth on art can be considered in two separate frameworks. In the relatively narrower frame; One can talk about the phenomenon's influence on artistic activities such as dance and music in India, or its influence on the birth of theater and other performing arts, as in the case of Dionysus. Additionally, when looking at the phenomenon from an iconographic and iconological perspective; It is certain that the depictions of Jesus in Christianity and Buddha in Buddhism offer such a rich inventory that they are the subject of a separate study in themselves[67].

However, based on all these findings, analyzes and interpretations in the previous section, a general evaluation can be made as follows:

If the phenomenon defined as the phenomenon of no-father birth is an effort to bring down a sacred (God)-centered sky and, in fact, the construction of the sacred system and hierarchy in the sky on earth, it becomes necessary to do on earth what the sacred and divine-otherworldly (God) does in the sky[68]. In this context, it is necessary to consider and interpret the activities

---

67 In both belief systems, especially in Christianity, this figural iconography constitutes the essence of decorative art.
68 What is meant here as sky should be perceived as cosmic, abstract, metaphysical and (or) spiritual.

of art and architecture[69] from this perspective, as well as all the actions of those who hold the authority of the sacred since the emergence of the idea of the state[70]. If the sacred (God) regulates the abstract-spiritual or cosmic, his son or representative (king, ruler, sultan, etc.) must also regulate the concrete. If God has a palace, a throne (seat), his son or representative must also have a throne, and if God's (holy) place is above, the buildings built in his name must be close to it[71]. If God is the greatest and most sublime as the holy one, the symbols that represent him must also be that great and sublime[72]. When the reality is viewed from

---

69 For the orders of the Ottoman sultans regarding the construction of buildings and the development of cities, see. Zeki Sönmez (1988). *Manuscripts-Documents About Mimar Sinan*, Istanbul: Mimar Sinan University Publications, p. 124-140.

70 Mircea Eliade, in his evaluations specifically about Babylonian architecture; He states that it is not possible to understand a ziggurat without considering it with a cosmic sky symbolism and argues that there is a relationship between the floors of the ziggurat and the parts of the universe. For detailed information, see Mircea Eliade (2002). Babylonian Cosmology and Alchemy, (Trans. Mehmet Emin Özcan), Istanbul: Kabalcı Publishing House, p. 26-32. It is possible to see this sky-temple relationship in Mesopotamia in the post-Islamic period. The Kaaba, the sacred structure of the Islamic religion, was considered by Muslims to be the highest structure (even though it was not high in terms of size) due to its location right opposite the pole star (Quoted by: Eliade, 2018b: 28). However, various shrines in many religions are directly associated with the unique figure of that religion. To give an example in this regard, a church beyond all its functions is, in terms of its planning, Jesus's; A Buddhist Stupa symbolizes the body of Buddha. For detailed information on the subject, see. Jale Nejdet Erzen (2017). *Habitus Trinity Earth,City,Structure*, İstanbul: YKY, p. 195-204.

71 In this context, a connection can be made between the king and the mausoleum tradition and from pyramids, which are high mausoleums, to tumuli, from mausoleums to burial grounds; It can be argued that there is an indirect relationship between holiness, temple and death.

72 For an alternative evaluation of the philosophical foundations of the perception of the sublime as sacred and its relationship with aesthetics, see. Immanuel Kant (2010). *Observations on the Feelings of Beauty and Sublimity*, (Trans. Ah-met Fethi), Istanbul: Hil Publications.

this perspective, it is possible to establish a relationship between the principles of formation and emergence of official and religious buildings, from their reasons for construction to their dimensions, from their programming to their decorations[73], and the phenomenon of no-father birth (in a perspective of at least five thousand years)[74]. (Photo 11, 12).

İsmail Tunalı, in the *Ontological Characteristics of Architectural Work* section of his work titled *Art Ontology*, explained this relationship (indirectly) as follows, depending on the definition of the metaphysical dimension[75] of the work:

These three layers are called the idea layer of the work of art. This layer is the farthest layer from the practical layer. Where the goal of the building work is an ideal goal, this inner layer meets the goal of the building work, as in temples, churches, cultural buildings, palaces and similar things. The ideal purpose of monumental structures is not identical with the human idea expressed in them. This can be clearly seen in the size of temples and churches. These are established in honor of certain Gods, but they transcend the ages; When there is no human being to bind them to a certain God, they still exist in

---

73 Even the non-ending fiction in ornamental arts can be evaluated in this context, and Selçuk Mülayim states that one of the general features of geometric ornaments in Anatolian Turkish Architecture is the principle of infinity (Mülayim, 1982: 70). Based on this, it is possible to think that there is a relationship between the perception of infinity, which is tried to be emphasized in an ornamentation program, and the unique infinite phenomenon (Photo 13).

74 In the Arab world, the connection with the sky and the impact of this connection on belief existed in the pre-Islamic period. Lat and Uzza, who were among the greatest deities of the pre-Islamic Arab society and whose names are mentioned in the Holy Quran, were goddesses associated with the sun and the sky. For pre-Islamic Arab belief, see. Murat Özcan (2018). "Arabic Mythology Before Islam", *Eastern and Western Mythologies*, Ankara: Delta Kitap, p. 15-24.

75 İsmail Tunalı named this metaphysical dimension as the third layer in his related work.

the same ideality; In other words, they are always felt as the expression of a greatness and will that goes beyond human scale. (Tunalı, 2014: 137, 138).

This feeling that İsmail Tunalı means can also be expressed as the spiritual aspect-dimension of the work of art, and according to this expression, art; It can be defined (in general terms) as the simultaneous[76] coming together of the spiritual and the sensory[77]. (Sözer, 2019: 5).

It is possible to see this approach, which was developed in the context of the relationship between the creation of a work of art and the phenomenon of no-father birth, within the understanding of art and architecture of the post-Islamic period (as the rulers are representatives of God).

He reveals His own image through man. As a matter of fact, the fact that man was created in the image of God means that God is a prototype of the human image. If virgin nature is the image of God, then man, who is at the center of this nature, must also be so; On the one hand, man witnesses the divine image that surrounds him, and on the other hand, when God takes human form, as in sacred art, he turns into this divine image. (Schuon, 2017: 51, 51).

---

76 The simultaneity emphasized here is the evaluation of what is and is not actually present, what is or is not contacted by sense organs, and, in a sense, what is and is not in this world, through a common perception. When we look at the issue from this perspective and in terms of architecture, structure can be defined as the transformation of the temporal into the spatial. For detailed information, see Onay Sözer (2019). *Art: The Invisible in the Visible*, Istanbul: YKY, p. 3-20.

77 Martin Heidegger defines human life in the world as a thrownness. When this theory of thrownness is considered with a focus on the thrown (coming-unknown) and the present-present place (world), a relationship can be established between the spiritual aspect of art and all kinds of human search for (truth), and the search can be interpreted as longing for the place arrived at. For detailed information, see. Martin Heidegger (2019). *What is the Reason*, (Trans. Saffet Babür), Ankara: Bilgesu Publications.

Photo 11: Great Stupa, 3rd Century AD, Sanchi/India, (Kandukuru Nagarjun).

Photo 12: Süleymaniye Mosque, 1550-1557, Istanbul.

Photo 13: Kayseri Ulu Mosque Pulpit, Under the Pavilion, 13th century.

Symbolism and Semiotics[78]

Based on the statements in the previous section, it can be seen that the relationship between the phenomenon of no-father birth and architecture is shaped around two determinants. One of these is symbolism and the other is semiotics. In this regard, it is necessary to focus on the relationship of both determinants with art and architecture.

It is a perfectly normal situation for the subconscious, which bears the traces of hundreds of years of experience, that an object that appeals to the human sense organs as great and sublime evokes God in human perception. Rudolf Otto emphasizes that the equivalent of numinous in art, which he sees as equivalent to the concept of God as the essence of the sacred, is specifically architecture, and its equivalent in architecture is magnificence, and he emphasizes that magnificence consists of three elements; He says that it is characterized by silence, darkness and emptiness (Otto, 2014: 100, 103). Edmund Burke says the following about the sublime and the techniques that create sublimity and its effect on personal perception:

As a result, any structure designed to evoke the notion of the sublime must be quite dim and gloomy for two reasons. In the first place, it is established by experience that darkness itself has a much

---

78 Part of this section of the book, Symbolism and Semiotics, is taken from the article Considerations on Belief, Architecture, and Perception. For the related article, see. Muzaffer Yilmaz (2017). "Considerations on Faith, Architecture and Perception", *Eskişehir Osmangazi University Journal of Social Sciences*, C: 18, P: 2, p. 67-92.

greater influence on the passions than light in other cases. Secondly, to make an object striking, we need to make it as different as possible from objects with which we are directly familiar. Therefore, when you enter a building, you cannot move from open air to brighter; Going into a place a few degrees darker may only make an insignificant change, but to make the transition completely striking, you need to go from the most light possible to the darkest possible state for the purposes of the architecture[79] (Burke, 2008: 85).

Here, the association of a work with anything else in human perception is related to its *purpose* other than its function, that is, its symbolic *connotation* other than the *Denotation* of architecture. *Denotation* is the first signified of a structure, that is, its function; *Connotation* can be defined as a phenomenon or symbolic message that is referred to outside of functionality (Eco, 2019: 28, 33). In this context, the structure becomes an *signified*. Signified is, in essence, a stimulus, and the image it evokes actually creates communication by indirectly connecting to another image[80] in the mind of the signified (Guiraud, 2016: 39). The important point at this point is that these symbolic expressions or indirect messages are important for the audience they address (sender-receiver). This *importance* is essentially related to the *culture* that connects the *signifier, signified* and the sent.

When we look at the issue specifically in Islamic Art; In general terms, it can be said that the main purpose of Islamic architecture is the desire to see the macrocosm in microcosm[81].

---

79 Light is the third tool used, along with geometry and rhythm, for the artist who wants to express the idea of the unity of existence (vahdat'ül vücûd) from an Islamic perspective. See Titus Burckhardt (2009). *Islamic Art Language and Meaning*, (Trans. Turan Koç), Istanbul: Klasik Publications, p. 112.
80 To give an example of this situation; Throne is literally a sitting object. However, in its connotation, it is not a sitting-resting area in the mind of the person who sees it, but a symbol of power-reign.
81 It should be noted that in the Islam-universe-architecture trilogy, the basic reference point of the subject is human.

The following words of the Islamic Caliph Ali are important to concretize the issue:

You think you are a small object, but the biggest universe is hidden in you (Quoted by: Kaya, 2011: 190).

Many scholars and wise men belonging to the school of Sufism have similar words. Mevlana celaleddin Rumi; *Man is God's astrolabe* (Mevlana Celaleddin Rumi, 1994: 17); Muhyiddin Ibn Arabi said; They emphasized this reality by saying that *The evidence for Allah is man* (Quoted by: De-mirli, 2014: 109).

In Islamic thought, there are opinions that even the ideal city, which is generally designed as a result of the intellectual perfection of the Islamic world, should have human characteristics and that just as the universe is manifested in humans, humans should also manifest themselves in the city. The great Islamic scholar Farabi says the following regarding the subject in his work titled El Medinet'ül Fazila (Ideal State):

The virtuous and perfect city resembles a complete and healthy body, all of whose organs cooperate with each other to make the life of the living being complete and to maintain it in this living state… and to the natural forces found in the organs of the body correspond the voluntary faculties and dispositions found in the parts of the city (Farabi, 2017: 98-100).

In parallel with this understanding, art (from an Islamic perspective) is an event that consists of the names belonging to the creator and revealed in the human being, which is the small universe, manifesting in itself and turning into reality. As a matter of fact, the prophet of Islam, Muhammad; He actually expresses this truth[82] by saying, *"When I looked at him, I did not see anything in him that did not make me think of God"* (Necmed-din-i Daye, 2013: 383, 384).

---

82 In this respect, the Western world and the Eastern world are at least partially separated from each other. Because in ancient Christian art, the aim was for everything to reach God (truth); In the east, God (truth) is intended to be visible in everything.

The combination of the perception that the whole is manifested in the part and the indirect expression style of art has given Islamic art an abstract nature that avoids direct imitation. Therefore, instead of imitating nature one-to-one (mimesis), Islamic artists turned to abstract elements in nature and produced products based on the sensitivity of monotheism and tanzih (Çaycı, 2016: 198). Considering that there is a high degree of abstraction in geometric shapes, it is possible to see an intense geometric repertoire in both Islamic architecture and decoration[83].

...Because it is not possible for us to comprehend and appreciate divinity through reasoning based on concepts and categories. The mind that works with concepts is a style of consciousness that comprehends the natural order. However, there is no value level in the natural order. The style of consciousness that comprehends the divine order is intuitive. The language that thinks closest to intuition is the symbolic language, which is a type of indirect expression. (Ögke, 2005: 25)

Apart from the buildings of the Islamic period, traces of the symbolic expression style, which emerged as a manifestation of a way of perceiving the world, can also be traced in the elements that make up the buildings. Minaret and finial are a good example of this. The first examples of minarets in Islamic architecture belong to the mosques of Kayravan (AD 726), Harran (AD 750) and Sa-marra (AD 852) (Bloom, 1989: 31,36,37,61). The high and tower-like minaret, on which the call to prayer is recited, is derived from the word *nur*, meaning light, and is the highest part of the temple that extends to the sky (in a way, to the sun-light).

---

83 For detailed information about Geometric Ornament in Islamic Art, see. Yıldız Demiriz (2001). Geometric Ornament in Islamic Art, Istanbul: Yo-rum Sanat Publications. For an in-depth study on geometric decoration in Ottoman Architecture, especially in Mimar Sinan's buildings, see. Serap Ekizler Sönmez and Aziz Doğanay (2015). "Square and Hexagonal Geometric Patterns in Mimar Sinan Mosques and Analysis Methods", *Turkish-Islamic Civilization Academic Research Journal*, No. 19, p. 87-108.

With these features, minarets are elegantly defined as; They can also be interpreted as the place of lighting the world with the Adhan of Muhammad, the place of illumination and istikhare (Cündioğlu, 2012: 25). The letter Elif is the place of unity in Islam and the name that belongs to it is trusteeship, which is to keep everything alive (Ibn Arabi, 2015: 86). Minarets, which are the architectural equivalent of the letter elif, which is the symbol of the position of proposal and unity in Islamic symbolism, are also the symbol of the adjective of majesty (Çaycı, 2017: 134, 136). There is a finial at the far end of the minaret, which is the closest part of the temple to the sky. The crescent located at the tip of the universe represents Allah in Islamic symbolism[84]. Additionally, Sâî Mustafa Çelebi, in his work titled Tezkiretü'l Bünyan and Tezki-retü'l Ebniye, consisting of the memoirs of Mimar Sinan, states that the world itself symbolizes Hz. Muhammad (Sai Mustafa Çelebi, 2003: 83). As can be seen, in Islamic architecture, minarets and finials, in terms of their principles of emergence, have deep symbolic meanings, far beyond their functionality, as they are the representations of the creator and the prophet (holy ones).

Establishing such a relationship between the structure and the element and the sacred is not a tradition specific to the Eastern Islamic world. For example, in Buddhism, object help has a very special place in a person's communication with God. According to ancient Indian teaching, all arts in the world could be achieved by imitating the devas (divine spirit-God). In parallel with this, stupas did not only function as grave monuments in Buddhism, they symbolized a model of the world and the body of Buddha for their believers (Eliade, 2004: 22, 23). Besides the temple itself being a manifestation and symbol of the divine spirit, for Hindus

---

84 According to Ebced calculation, the numerical values of both words are 66. For detailed information about Ebced Account, see. Ramazan Ayçiçek (2004). "Cefr and Ebced-Metaphysics of Letters and Numbers in Terms of Information Value", *Milel and Nihal (Journal of Faith Culture and Mythology Research)*, Y: 2, S: 1, p. 75-114.

the temple was also a place where God was visible (Michell, 1988: 61). In this context, the roadside temples, which are called *mandir* (waiting place), *prasada* (place of grace) or *devalaya* (house of God) and are widely seen throughout the Hindu geography, are noteworthy (Photo 14). It is believed that these roadside temples, which Hindus mostly call mandirs, which can be seen on the side of a road or on a sidewalk, and even have mobile versions, are (still) the earthly home of God and that he awaits his worshipers here (Öztürk , 2019: 17). Even the construction of cathedrals in medieval Europe in the center of the city required a similar approach, and these structures were undoubtedly not the result of an initiative related only to the construction of a lofty structure.

Medieval people lived in a world full of intuitive facts and descriptions, looking for a connection with God in everything (Eco, 2016: 96). Dante, the important writer and thinker of the 13th century, actually summarizes the worldview of this period by saying that *the apparent and visible meanings are just a cover* (Quoted by: Guenon, 2014: 9). In this world that has meaning beyond what it seems, architecture did not only have functional concerns. The size of a Gothic cathedral not only allowed it to accommodate many believers, but also continued the tradition of the Bronze Age with its majesty that tried to emulate the sky, and created a perception of sublimity on people (Photo 15). In fact, it can be said that faith, in a way, was attempting to manage perception with all the possibilities of architecture. Even the fantastic creatures we see on the exteriors of medieval cathedrals actually served a similar purpose, giving an allegorical message that evil is outside the church (Photo 16).

In addition to all these inferences and comments; It is also necessary to mention the obsession with high, large and ornate objects, which has become a kitsche in today's Islamic world. These contemporary practices, which are good examples of confusing sublimity with height and elegance with wealth, do not actually serve the functionality mission of architecture, but are concerned with a purely ostentatious attitude (dirigism). An important question that should be mentioned at this point is whether the mentality that creates these show-oriented structures, which cannot stop associating sublimity with height despite the fact that the sacred phenomenon has changed its identity, has anything to do with the traces left in our subconscious by the thoughts mentioned in the previous pages[85] (Photo 17).

Photo 14: A Roadside Temple, Undated, Kathmandu/Nepal (Nermin Öztürk)

---

85 For an interesting study on the relationship between the subconscious and belief, see. Talat, Parman (2018). "Myth, Legend, Epic, Story, Narrative, Word, Discourse. So Why Do We Tell It?", *Psychomythology, Searching for People in Their Stories*, (Ed. M. Bilgin Saydam and Hakan Kızıltan), Istanbul: İthaki Publications.

Photo 15: York Cathedral, 13-15. Century, York/England.

Photo 16: Notre Dame Cathedral Detail, 12-14. Century, Paris/France.

Photo 17: Kaaba and Its Surroundings, 2017, Mecca / Saudi Arabia, (Konya Selçuklu Municipality).

Foundation Institution as an Architectural Activity and Symbol

The word *foundation* is derived from the Arabic word *'vakafe'* ( ), which means 'to stand'; It is used in the sense of allocating a property in perpetuity for the public benefit (Pakalın, 1993: 577). With the foundation deed, which is the document prepared to concretize this intention and realize the allocation process, the intention was made official and functional at the same time (Photo 18). The origin of the foundation institution goes back to the Islamic prophet Muhammad, from a religious perspective, and to the Sumerian and Babylonian civilizations, from a historical perspective (Hatemi, 1985: 1660). However, a functional, ideal and institutional foundation institution is fully seen in the Seljuk and Ottoman periods. Foundations, which are institutions in which an entity was created for purposes other than its own, without profit and to gain the consent of God, constituted one of the most important dynamics of cultural life as well as socio-economic life, especially in the Seljuk and Ottoman states. The foundation tradition, which was accepted as a prophetic practice (charity) within the Turkish-Islamic tradition, was considered a duty[86] primarily for the rulers and later

---

86 Undoubtedly, it should be noted that the establishment of the foundation institution is not only based on religious concerns and pure feelings. Establishing a foundation, especially for someone working at the state level, meant preventing their property from being confiscated by the state in the event of a possible dismissal. From this perspective, it can be thought that foundations, in a way, also function to smuggle property and money.

for the ruling family and their surroundings. In this respect, especially in Ottoman architecture, it is seen that many buildings built under state control were built as foundation works. Within this understanding, it is seen that sometimes a single fountain or dispenser, and sometimes huge social complexes consisting of buildings, were built as foundation works.

Ahmet Çaycı defines foundations as a combination of values such as *philanthropic-ethics* and *beauty-aesthetics* (Çaycı, 2018: 268). With the concept of ihsan, Çaycı emphasizes the principle of charity, which has morality at its core, and with the concept of beauty, he emphasizes a universal understanding of beauty. It is certain that the foundation provides the person with a state of satisfaction in accordance with his belief, in relation to its *philanthropic-ethical* understanding. However, these practices are mostly related[87] to the ruler (sultan-ruler) and his environment; Depending on the desire and goal[88] of goodness to last forever (eternity), it shows that the foundation institution is indirectly, if not directly, related to the phenomenon of no-father birth mentioned in the study. In other words; Although all development activities that can be considered official have completely different purposes and functions (enabling people to worship,

---

In addition, the fact that foundations were exempt from taxes sometimes created a negative economic situation for the state. However, it must be said that foundations were extremely important for the Ottoman Empire for many centuries, considering both the employment they created and the activities they carried out on behalf of the state. In the modern world and with the development of banking, foundation institutions have largely lost their mission in the eyes of the state.

87 In the 18th century, foundations belonging to the civil servant class affiliated with the palace constituted an 80% share in the Ottoman foundation system (Yediyıldız, 1982: 160). In the Seljuks, although only 12% of the total foundations belonged to the sultans, the proportion of foundations belonging to the umera class and the Ahis, who were associated with the ruling party, was 63% (Yüksel, 2006: 310).

88 In this context, there is a similarity with the understanding and quest for universal beauty expressed by Ahmet Çaycı.

receive education, or providing water, etc.), in fact, in line with what is claimed in this study, it is an imitation of the system of the only eternal sacred (God). It is an attempt to resist eternity (time) with architecture (space), as a duty, with the inevitable knowledge of mortality..

As can be seen, there is much that can be said about the foundation institution, which is one of the main fields of study in history as well as economics, sociology, theology and art history.

Photo 18: An Example of Foundation Deed (Ahmet Çaycı)

Phenomenon of Sacred Birth

After talking about sacred figures born from an earthly mother and the relationship of this phenomenon in the faith-religion-state-art quadrilateral (even though this issue is partially touched upon in the forty-fourth footnote), we talk about a god and goddess, or abstract-sacred beings. It would be appropriate to briefly mention the phenomenon of *holy virgin birth*.

In many myths in the geographies where fatherless births are seen, which are discussed in the Examples of the Phenomenon section, there are divinities born from gods and goddesses or abstract-sacred beings, some of whom also emphasize virginity, but who may have worldly authority (authority). There are sacred figures. For example, according to Egyptian Mythology, Seth, the brother of God Osiris who was jealous of Osiris for making his country prosperous (some sources state that Osiris held a grudge against him because he was with Seth's wife), set a trap for his brother and put him in a sarcophagus. He imprisons him, kills him, and throws the sarcophagus into the Nile River. After the sarcophagus hits the ground, a tree encases Osiris inside the sarcophagus. After a while, the columns made of this tree were used in the construction of a palace, and Goddess Isis, who went to search for her husband, went to this palace, found her husband's body, and on the way back, she got pregnant from his corpse and gave birth to God Horus (Photo 19)[89].

---

89 The story is briefly told here. For detailed information, see Donna Rosenberg (2000). *World Mythology Great Epics and Legends Anthology*, (Trans. Koray Akten, Erdal Cengiz, et al.), Istanbul: İmge Kitabevi, p. 261-270.

Joseph Campbell states that numerous sacred[90] births encountered in different mythologies and bearing similar characteristics to this example are not biological, but spiritual births related to spiritual development-evolution[91] (Campbell and Moyers, 2007: 225, 227).

The next, fourth center is at heart level; This region is the area of opening to love. Here you leave the realm of animal action and enter a very human, spiritual realm. When we awaken to love, compassion, shared pain at the heart level, when we share the pain of another person, this is the beginning of humanity. Religious thought begins at this level, the heart level (Campbell and Moyers, 2007: 225.)

The findings of Nermin Öztürk, who interprets the phenomenon of holy and virgin birth in a similar way from a broad perspective, are also very important at this point:

As we emphasize in the text, one of those who gave a virgin birth was Hz. Muhammad. He is both "ummi" and "rahim". What arises from it is the "Divine Word". This situation is the most important evidence that virgin birth should be perceived metaphorically. But in no religion or mythology is the virgin birth story told through a man. No man can be associated with the concept of either fertility or breastfeeding. Because fertility, ontologically, is a privilege granted by God to the female sex. These directly evoke the female gender in the human mind. However, in Eliade's words, what is tried to be expressed with "woman" in myths and rituals is not a biological woman but a cosmic principle. Therefore, when it

---

90 Researchers such as Campbell did not separate sacred births from virgin births and accepted them as part of a whole. In this regard, while there is no virginity in some examples, motifs of virginity or getting pregnant without intercourse can be seen in some examples.

91 Campbell states that this symbolic expression is a common language. This common language or the same symbolic expression that emerges in different cultures and societies is actually related to the functions of mythology that he stated in another of his works. See Joseph Campbell (2014). *Creative Mythology Masks of God*, C: 4, (Trans. Kudret Emiroğlu), Istanbul: Islık Yayınları, p. 13-19.

comes to religious texts, one should not make the mistake of superficially understanding the concepts with their concrete meanings. What is tried to be expressed here is a theoretical and metaphysical dimension. This cosmic feminine principle, expressed with the words prakriti and shakti in the Hindu tradition and yin in the Chinese teaching, found its equivalent in the Quran with the word uns (Hucurat, 13), but none other than the Sufis focused on this and preferred to understand the word in its literal sense. Mystics, on the other hand, used this cosmic principle as the soul. As a cosmic principle, masculinity and femininity are principles that exist within every biological human being. Therefore, the characteristics of fertility and motherhood are potentials that exist in everyone's spirituality, regardless of their gender roles. It is up to humans to reveal these[92]. (Öztürk, 2020: 181, 182).

It is understood from both Campbell and Öztürk's approaches that; *The virgin born of the cosmic-spiritual world (faith), which can be considered as the forerunner of the fatherless born saints who emerged as a political-religious figure,* is essentially one of the most important and effective symbolic narratives in the history of faith[93]. From this perspective, *the phenomenon of no-father birth* as tried to be explained in this book; It can be accepted as the way in which a *spiritual evolution-leap* that is tried to be expressed *symbolically* as the *subject of belief* has been changed, interpreted and manipulated by the *phenomena of religion and state* in order to establish and maintain a *social-political institutional* structure.

---

92 According to Eliade, man is capable of establishing a spiritual-intuitive communication with the sacred because he is homo religious and homo symbolicus. According to Evelyn Underhill, this feature of humans is related to the divine origin of the human soul (Underhill, 2003: 83).

93 The fact that the same story-narrative or what is intended to be told-message differs according to cultures, and the change in icons and symbols can be explained by the fact that cultural codes differ according to geographies. For a similar motif that changes according to cultural codes and geography, see. Nermin Öztürk (2013). *The Changing Face of the Sacred, From Lion Goddesses to Lion Saints*, Konya: Ideal Usta Publications.

Photo 19: Isis and Horus, 332-330 BC, Metropolitan Museum of Art, (https://www.metmuseum.org/).

At The End

A large part of the studies that have been done and are being carried out on art history consist of descriptive research and studies. However, symbolism has recently become a concept that has been mentioned and emphasized in many studies on art history. It is seen that the subject is frequently discussed by researchers from the faculties of theology and fine arts, especially within the scope of Islamic art. However, the subject of Islamic art and symbolism; It is obvious that there is a need for broad-perspective comparisons, interdisciplinary approaches and deeper evaluations, apart from shallow approaches consisting of clichés such as *the point is Allah and everything comes from that Allah* and based on (mere) religious literal knowledge.

As someone who thinks that it is necessary to question a hermeneutical religion-art practice[94], especially in the context of art history, outside of symbolism as a concept but also including it, I believe that research related to these questions should only

---

94 In this context, the main issue that needs to be mentioned is the aspect of religion that enables this relationship. In this respect, although hermetic thought (and way of thinking) is an area that needs to be seriously focused on, it has not been explained and the relationship of the subject with art has been left to another separate publication in order not to branch out too much and not to expand the range of meaning of the subject. Regarding hermetic thought, see. Mahmud Erol Kılıç (2017). *Hermes of Hermes, Hermes and Hermetic Thought in the Light of Islamic Sources*, Istanbul: Sufi Kitap Publications; İzzet Erş (2019). *Interpretation of the Sacred, Hermeneutic Essays on Sacred Texts*, Istanbul: Siyah Kitap Publications.

be carried out in art. I argue that it should benefit from the inventory of many different disciplines and fields such as history or theology, but also history, philosophy, political science, mythology, anthropology, sociology and cinema. In this context, I would especially like to point out that research and the studies that will emerge based on research should be process-oriented, not result-oriented. This book, written in this manner, is very suitable for expansion in many aspects, even though it does not have a large number of pages.

Commentary brings the text to life. It is the interpreter's ability to reveal, open and spread what is intended to be said in the text (the intention of the text) in his own language. Within the open space of interpretation, texts reveal their own existence. According to Gadamer, interpretation is not a simple repetition or reproduction of the text in this respect; It is the fusion of the meaning horizon of the text and the meaning horizon of the interpreter. In other words, it is the participation of the interpreter of the text in the game as a player in the world of meaning. After all, the act of interpretation is a kind of playing a game. It is a kind of game that takes place between the text's possible perspectives and the interpreter's previous perspectives on a common subject or field, the outcome of which is unpredictable and the text and the commentator share. (Tatar, 2016: 67).

I hope that this game, which I play based on my own search for meaning, will raise awareness among its interlocutors and be conducive to those who want to work on similar subjects...

It is possible to get stuck in the outside world and think that everything is there. When you think of Jesus, you have feelings about how he suffered there. But this pain must continue within you too. Have you been spiritually reborn? Have you killed your animal nature and come back to life as the human embodiment of love?

Joseph Campbell

REFERANCES

Print:

Akoğulları, Mehmet Ali ve Köker, Levent (2017). *İmparatorluktan Tanrı Devletine*, İstanbul: İmge Kitabevi.

Akoğulları, Mehmet Ali ve Köker, Levent (2018). *Kral-Devlet ya da Ölümlü Tanrı*, İstanbul: İmge Kitabevi.

Akgezer, Bülent (2018). *Dionysos Özgürlüğün Şarkısı*, İstanbul: Yitik Ülke Yayınları.

Akurgal, Ekrem (2005). *Anadolu Kültür Tarihi*, Ankara: TÜBİTAK Yayınları.

Altındal, Aytunç (2018). *Hangi İsa Tyanalı Apollonius*, İstanbul: Destek Yayınları.

Altunay, Erhan (2014). *Paganizm-I Kadim Bilgeliğe Giriş*, İstanbul: Hermes Yayınları.

Altuncu, Abdullah (2014). "Sümer Mitolojisi Bağlamında Otorite Tarafından Şekillendirilen İbadet ve Törenler", *Kilis 7 Aralık Üniversitesi İlahiyat Fakültesi Dergisi*, C: 1, S: 1, s. 141-165.

Armstrong, Karen (2017). *Tanrı'nın Tarihi*, (Çev. Oktay Özel, Hamide Koyukan, Kudret Emiroğlu), İstanbul: Pegasus Yayınları.

Armstrong, Karen (2019). *Büyük Dönüşüm Eksen Çağı ve Dinsel Geleneklerim Başlangıcı*, İstanbul: Pegasus Yayınları.

Ashkenazi, Michael (2003). *Japon Mitolojisi*, (Çev. Özlem Özarpacı), İstanbul: Say Yayınları.

Ayçiçek, Ramazan (2004). "Bilgi Değeri Açısından Cefr ve Ebced -Harfler ve Rakamlar Metafiziği-", *Milel ve Nihal (İnanç Kültür ve Mitoloji Araştırmaları Dergisi)*, Y: 2, S: 1, s. 75-114.

Bachofen, Jacob (2019). *Söylence, Din ve Anaerki*, (Çev. Nilgün Şarman), İstanbul: Payel Yayınevi.

Bahadır, Abdülkerim (2018). *İnsanın Anlam Arayışı ve Din*, İstanbul: İsyan Yayınları.

Barnard, Alan (2016). *Simgesel Düşüncenin Doğuşu*, (Çev. Mehmet Doğan), İstanbul: Boğaziçi Üniversitesi Yayınları.

Balcıoğlu, Merve (2018). "Japonya'da Kamu Yönetimi ve Japon Siyasal Kültürünün Özgün Yanları", *Turkish Studies*, C: 11, S: 56, s. 709-719.

Berger, L. Peter (2015). *Kutsal Şemsiye Dinin Sosyolojik Teorisinin Ana Unsurları*, (Çev. Ali Coşkun), İstanbul: Rağbet Yayınları.

Bilican, Rukiye (2017). *Hint Danslarının Dini Temeli*, Yüksek Lisans Tezi, Marmara Üniversitesi Sosyal Bilimler Enstitüsü, Ankara.

Bloom, Jonathan (1989). Minaret *Symbol of Islam*, Oxforf: Oxford University Press.

Bose, R. Ramasvami (2016). *Hint Mitolojisi*, (Çev. Namık Çetin), İstanbul: Mitoloji Tarihi Yayınları.

Boudieu, Pierre (2019). *Eril Tahakküm*, (Çev. Bediz Yılmaz), İstanbul: Bağlam Yayınları.

Bulut, Gülden (2014). *Mitolojik Astroloji ve Psikoloji*, İzmir: Zodyak Astroloji Yayınları.

Bulut, Gülden (2018). *Gökyüzünün Söyledikleri*, İzmir: Zodyak Astroloji Yayınları.

Burckhardt, Titus (2009). *İslam Sanatı Dil ve Anlam*, (Çev. Turan Koç), İstanbul: Klasik Yayınları.

Burckhardt, Titus (2017). *Doğu'da Batı'da Kutsal Sanat*, (Çev. Tahir Uluç), İstanbul: İnsan Yayınları.

Burke, Edmund (2008). *Yüce ve Güzel Kavramlarımızın Kaynağı Hakkında Felsefi Bir Soruşturma*, (Çev. M. Barış Gümüşbaş), Ankara: Bilgesu Yayıncılık.

Campbell, Joseph ve Moyers Bill (2007). *Mitolojinin Gücü, Kutsal Kitaplardan Hollywood Filmlerine Mitoloji ve Hikayeleri*, (Çev. Zeynep Yaman), İstanbul: MediaCat Kitapları.

Campbell, Joseph (201). *Yaratıcı Mitoloji Tanrının Maskeleri*, C: 4, (Çev. Kudret Emiroğlu), İstanbul: Islık Yayınları.

Campbell, Joseph (2015). *Batı Mitolojisi Tanrının Maskeleri*, C: 3, (Çev. Kudret Emiroğlu), İstanbul: Islık Yayınları.

Campbell, Joseph (2016). *Doğu Mitolojisi*, C: 2, (Çev. Kudret Emiroğlu), İstanbul: Islık Yayınları.

Campbell, Joseph (2019). *Kahramanın Sonsuz Yolculuğu*, (Çev. Sabri Gürses), İstanbul: İthaki Yayınları.

Collins, Andrew (2017). *Göbekli Tepe Tanrıların Doğuşu*, (Çev. Leyla Tonguç Basmacı), İstanbul: Alfa Yayınları.

Coomaraswamy, Ananda Kentish (2016). "Hristiyan Doğulu Veya Gerçek Sanat Felsefesi", *Her İnsan Sanatçı Doğar*, İstanbul: İnsan Yayınları, s. 107-141.

Corbin, Henry (2016). *Tanrının Yüzü İnsanın Yüzü Yorumbilgisi ve Tasavvuf*, (Çev. Kübra Gürkan ve B. Garen Beşiktaşlıyan), İstanbul: Pinhan Yayınları.

Cündioğlu, Dücane (2012). *Mimarlık ve Felsefe*, İstanbul: Kapı Yayınları.

Çaycı, Ahmet (2016). "İslam Mimarisinde Anlam Meselesi", *Sosyoloji Divanı*, Sayı: 7, s.189-202.

Çaycı, Ahmet (2017). *İslam Mimarisinde Anlam ve Sembol*, Konya: Palet Yayınları.

Çaycı, Ahmet (2018). *Türk-İslam Kültüründe Vakıf ve Sanat*, Konya: Palet Yayınları.

Çaycı, Ahmet (2019). *Anadolu Selçuklu Sanatı'nda Gezegen ve Burç Tasvirleri*, Konya: Palet Yayınları.

Çığ, Muazzez İlmiye (2011). *İnanna'nın Aşkı Sümer'de İnanç ve Kutsal Evlenme*, İstanbul: Kaynak Yayınları.

Çığ, Muazzez İlmiye (2019). *Bereket Kültü ve Mabed Fahişeliği*, İstanbul: Kaynak Yayınları.

Demirli, Ekrem (2014). "Tasavvufta Estetik Algısı Hakkında Bir Değerlendirme", *VI. Dini Yayınlar Kongresi -İslam Sanat ve Estetik- (29 Kasım- 01 Aralık 2013)*, Bildiri Kitabı, İstanbul: Diyanet İşleri Başkanlığı Yayınları, s. 105-110.

Demiriz, Yıldız (2001). *İslam Sanatında Geometrik Süsleme*, İstanbul: Yorum Sanat Yayınları.

Detienne, Mareel, (2010). "Dionysos Maddesi", *Mitolojiler Sözlüğü*, (Çev. Nusat Çıka), (Yön. Yves Bonneffoy, Türkçe Yay. Haz. Levent Yılmaz), C: 1, Ankara: Dost Kitabevi Yayınları, s. 172-179.

Durkheim, Emile (2005). *Dini Hayatın İlkel Biçimleri*, (Çev. Fuat Aydın), İstanbul: Ataç Yayınları.

Eco, Umberto (2016). *Ortaçağ Estetiğinde Sanat ve Güzellik*, (Çev. Kemal Atakay), İstanbul: Can Yayınları.

Eco, Umberto (2019). *Mimarlık Göstergebilimi*, (Çev. Fatma Erkman Akerson), İstanbul: Daimon Yayınları.

Eliade, Mircea (2002). *Babil Kozmolojisi ve Simyası*, (Çev. Mehmet Emin Özcan), İstanbul: Kabalcı Yayınevi.

Eliade, Mircea (2004). *Mistik Hint Erotizmi*, (Çev. Renan Akman), İstanbul: Kabalcı Yayıları.

Eliade, Mircea (2014). *Dinler Tarihine Giriş*, (Çev. Lale Arslan Özcan), İstanbul: Kabalcı Yayınları.

Eliade, Mircea (2016). *Okültizm, Büyücülük ve Kültürel Modalar* (Çev. Cem Soydemir), İstanbul: DOĞUBATI Yayınları.

Eliade, Mircea (2018a). *Dinsel İnançlar ve Düşünceler Tarihi*, (Çev. Ali Berktay), C: 1, İstanbul: Alfa Yayınları.

Eliade, Mircea (2018b). *Ebedi Dönüş Miti*, (Çev. Ayşe Meral), İstanbul: Dergah Yayınları.

Eliade, Mircea (2019). *Dinsel İnançlar ve Düşünceler Tarihi*, (Çev. Ali Berktay), C: 2, İstanbul: Alfa Yayınları.

Ergin, Muharrem (2003). *Göktürk Kitabeleri*, İstanbul: Boğaziçi Yayınları.

Erş, İzzet (2019). *Kutsalın Yorumu Kutsal Metinler Üzerine Hermenötik Denemeler*, İstanbul: Siyah Kitap Yayınları.

Erzen, Jale Nejdet (2017). *Üç Habitus Yeryüzü Kent Yapı*, İstanbul: YKY.

Farabi (2017). *İdeal Devlet*, (Çev. Ahmet Arslan), İstanbul: İş Bankası Yayınları.

Farthing, Stephen (2017). *Sanatın Tüm Öyküsü*, (Çev. Gizem Aldoğan ve Firdevs Candil Çulcu), İstanbul: Hayalperest Yayınları.

Frangipane, Marcela (2002). *Yakındoğu'da Devletin Doğuşu*, (Çev. Z. Zühre İlkgelen), İstanbul: Arkeoloji Sanat Yayınları.

Frazer, James George (1917). *The Golden Bough A Study In Magic And Religion (Part I The Magic Art Evolution Of Kings)*, C: 2, London: Macmillan and Co., Limited Press.

Frazer, James George (2016). *Altın Dal Dinin ve Folklorun Kökenleri*, (Çev. Mehmet H. Doğan), İstanbul: Yapı Kredi Yayınları.

Frazer, James George (2018). *Adonis, Attis, Osiris Doğu Dinleri Tarihi Araştırmaları I*, (Çev. İsmail Hakkı Yılmaz), İstanbul: Pinhan Yayınları.

Gibson, Clare (2016). *Semboller Nasıl Okunur*, (Çev. Cem Alpan), İstanbul: YEM Yayınları.

Gimbutas, Marija (2001). *The Living Goddesses*, California: University of California Press.

Grimal, Pierre (2012). *Mitoloji Sözlüğü Yunan Roma*, (Çev. Sevgi Tamgüç), İstanbul: Kabalcı Yayınları.

Guenon, Rene (2014). *Dante ve Orta Çağ'da Dini Sembolizm*, (Çev. İsmail Taşpınar), İstanbul: İnsan Yayınları.

Guenon, Rene (2017). *Yatay ve Dikey Boyutların Sembolizmi*, (Çev. Fevzi Topaçoğlu), İstanbul: İnsan Yayınları.

Guiraud, Pierre (2016). *Göstergebilim*, (Çev. Mehmet Yalçın), İstanbul: İmge Kitabevi.

Gül, Ali (2018). *Ansiklopedik Hinduzim Sözlüğü*, İstanbul: İz Yayınları.

Gündüz, Şinasi, Ünal, Yavuz ve Sandıkçıoğlu Ekrem (1996). *Dinlerde Yükseliş Motifleri*, Ankara: Vadi Yayınları.

Gündüz, Şinasi (1998). *Mitoloji İle İnanç Arasında Ortadoğu ve Dinsel Gelenekleri Üzerine Yazılar*, Samsun: Etüt Yayınları.

Halis, Göktuğ (2016). *Simgebilim Perspektifinden Göbeklitepe Tapınakları*, İstanbul: Ozan Yayıncılık.

Harman, Ömer Faruk (2010). "Süleyman Maddesi", *TDV İslam Ansiklopedisi*, Ankara: TDV Yayınları, C: 38, s. 60-62.

Harman, Ömer Faruk (2017). "Beklenen Kurtarıcı İnancının İslam Öncesi Arka Planı", *Beklenen Kurtarıcı İnancı*, İstanbul: KURAMER Yayınları, s. 41-59.

Harva, Ono (2014). *Altay Panteonu Mitler Ritüeller İnançlar ve Tanrılar*, (Çev. Ömer Suveren), İstanbul: Doğu Kütüphanesi Yayınları.

Hatemi, Hüseyin (1985). "Tanzimat'tan Cumhuriyet'e Vakıf", *Tanzimat'tan Cumhuriyet'e Türkiye Ansiklopedisi*, C: 6, İstanbul: İletişim Yayınları, s. 1658-1679.

Heidegger, Martin (2019). *Nedenin Neliği*, (Çev. Saffet Babür), Ankara: Bilgesu Yayınları.

Hornoung, Erik (2014). *Mısır Bilimine Giriş*, (Çev. Zehra Aksu Yılmazer), İstanbul: Kabalcı Yayınları.

İbn Arabi (2015). *Harflerin Esrarı*, (Çev. Ekrem Demirli), İstanbul: Litera Yayınları.

İpşirli, Mehmet (2012). "Unvan Maddesi Osmanlılar", *TDV İslam Ansiklopedisi*, C: 42, s.166.

Anonim, *İhvan-ı Safa Risaleleri*, (Çev. A. Karaman, İ. Çalışkan, E. Uysal, A. Avcu, M. Demirkol, K. Göktay ve E. Aliyev), C: 2, İstanbul: Ayrıntı Yayınları.

Jung, Carl Gustave (2004). *Eşzamanlılık: Nedensellik Dışı Bağlayıcı Bir İlke*, (Çev. Levent Özşar), Bursa: Bilos Yayınları.

Jung, Carl Gustave (2016). *İnsan ve Sembolleri*, (Çev. Hatice Mukaddes İlgün), İstanbul: Kabalcı Yayınları.

Kalın, Fettullah (2014). *Rudolf Otto'da Din, Kutsallık ve Mistik Tecrübe*, İstanbul: Ötüken Yayınları.

Kant, Immanuel (2010). *Güzellik ve Yücelik Duyguları Üzerine Gözlemler*, (Çev. Ahmet Fethi), İstanbul: Hil Yayınları.

Kaya, Murat (2011). *Hz Ali'den 111 Hatıra*, İstanbul: Erkam Yayınları.

Keskin, Mustafa (2004). "Din ve Toplum İlişkileri Üzerine Bir Genelleme", *Din Bilimleri Akademik Araştırma Dergisi*, C: 4, S: 2, s. 7-21.

Kılıç, Mahmud Erol (2017). *Hermeslerin Hermesi İslam Kaynakları Işığında Hermes ve Hermetik Düşünce*, İstanbul: Sufi Kitap Yayınları.

Klengel, Horst (2019). *Kral Hammurabi ve Babil Günlüğü*, (Çev. Nesri Oral), Ankara: Totem Yayınları.

Kramer, Samuel Noah (2002). *Tarih Sümer'de Başlar*, (Çev. Hamide Koyukan), İstanbul: Kabalcı Yayınları.

Küçükaşcı, Mustafa Sabri (2009). "Seyyid Maddesi", *TDV İslam Ansiklopedisi*, Ankara: TDV Yayınları, C: 37, s. 40-43.

Leeming, David (2001). *A Dictionary of Asian Mythology*, New York: Oxford University Press.

Leeming, David Adams (2018). *A'dan Z'ye Dünya Mitolojisi*, (Çev. Nurdan Sosyal), İstanbul: SAY Yayınları.

Leeming, David, ve Page, Jake (2019). *Tanrıça Mitleri*, (Çev. Şükrü Alpagut), Say Yayınları: İstanbul.

Mevlana Celaleddin (1994). *Fîhi Mâfih*, (Çev. A. Avni Konuk), (Yay. Haz. S. Eraydın), İstanbul: İz Yayınları.

Michell, George (1988). *The Hindu Temple: An Introduction to Its Meaning and Form*, Chicago: University of Chicago Press.

Mülayim, Selçuk (1982). *Anadolu Türk Mimarisinde Geometrik Süsleme*, Ankara: Kültür Bakanlığı Yayınları.

Nanamoli, Bhikkhu (2001). *The Life of Buddha*, Onalaska (USA): BPE Press.

Nasr, Seyyid Hüseyin (2017). *İslam Sanatı ve Maneviyatı*, (Çev. Ahmet Demirhan), İstanbul: İnsan Yayınları.

Necmeddin-i Daye (2013). *Mirsadü'l-İbad*, (Çev. Halil Baltacı), İstanbul: İFAV Yayınları.

Ocak, Ahmet Yaşar (2012). *Türk İslam İnançlarında Hızır Yahut Hızır İlyas Kültü*, İstanbul: Kabalcı Yayınları.

Okumuş, Ejder (2005). *Dinin Meşrulaştırma Gücü*, İstanbul: ARK Yayınları.

Otto, Rudolf (2014). *Kutsal'a Dair*, (Çev. Sevil Ghaffari), İstanbul: Altıkırkbeş Yayınları.

Ovidius (1994). *Dönüşümler*, (Çev. İsmet Zeki Eyüboğlu), İstanbul: Payel Yayınları.

Ögke, Ahmet (2005). *Türk Tasavvuf Düşüncesinde Metaforik Anlatım*, Van: Ahenk Yayınları.

Özcan, Murat (2018). "İslamiyet'ten Önce Arap Mitolojisi", *Doğu ve Batı Mitolojileri*, Ankara: Delta Kitap, s. 15-24.

Öztürk, Nermin (2013). *Kutsalın Değişen Yüzü Aslanlı Tanrıçalardan Aslanlı Erenlere*, Konya: İdeal Usta Yayınları.

Öztürk, Nermin (2019). "Hindu Halk Dindarlığının Merkezindeki Yapılar: Yol Kenarı Tapınakları", *Çukurova Üniversitesi İlahiyat Fakültesi Dergisi*, C: 19, S: 1, s. 16-32.

Öztürk, Nermin (2020). *Budizm'de, Hıristiyanlık'ta ve İslam'da Bakire Doğum Fenomolojik Bir Yaklaşım*, Konya: Literatürk-Academia Yayınları.

Parman, Talat (2018). "Mit, Efsane, Destan, Hikaye, Anlatı, Söz, Söylem Sahi Neden Anlatıyoruz ?", *Psikomitoloji İnsanı Öykülerinde Aramak*, (Ed. M. Bilgin Saydam ve Hakan Kızıltan), İstanbul: İthaki Yayınları.

Özaydın, Abdülkerim (2012). "Unvan Maddesi", *TDV İslam Ansiklopedisi*, C: 42, s. 163-166

Pakalın, Mehmet Zeki (1993). *Osmanlı Tarih Deyimleri ve Terimleri Sözlüğü*, C: 3, İstanbul: MEB Yayınları.

Pattanaik, Devdutt (2006). *Hint Mitolojisine Giriş Mit ve Mitya*, (Çev. Çiğdem Erkal), İstanbul: Doğubatı Yayınları.

Renou, Louis (2016). *Hinduizm*, (Çev. Maide Selen), İstanbul: İletişim Yayınları.

Roth, Lenand Martin (2002). *Mimarlığın Öyküsü*, İstanbul: Kabalcı Yayınları.

Rosenberg, Donna (2000). *Dünya Mitolojisi Büyük Destanlar ve Söylenceler Antolojisi*, (Çev. Koray Akten, Erdal Cengiz, A. Ulaş Yüce, Kudret Emiroğlu, Tuluğ Kenanoğlu, Tahir Kocayiğit, Erhan Kuzhan, Bengü Odabaşı), İstanbul: İmge Kitabevi.

Sâî Mustafa Çelebi (2003). *Tezkiretü'l-Bünyan ve Tezkiretü'l-Ebniye*, (Yay. Haz. Hayati Develi), İstanbul: KOÇ Kültür Sanat Tanıtım.

Sarıkçıoğlu, Ekrem (2011). *Din Fenomenolojisi*, Isparta: Fakülte Kitabevi.

Sheldrake, Rupert (2001). *Yeni Bir Yaşam Bilimi*, (Çev. Sezer Soner), İzmir: Ege-Meta Yayınları.

Sheldrake, Rupert (2004). *Biri Beni Gözetliyor*, (Çev. Orhan Düz), İstanbul: Kaknüs Yayınları.

Schimmel, Annamaria (1999). *Dinler Tarihine Giriş*, İstanbul: Kırkambar Yayınları.

Schmidt, Klaus (2007). *Göbekli Tepe En Eski Tapınağı Yapanlar*, İstanbul: Arkeoloji Sanat Yayınları.

Shoun, Frithjof (2016). *Bir Merkeze Sahip Olmak*, (Çev. Tahir Uluç), İstanbul: İnsan Yayınları.

Schuon, Frithjof (2017). *Beşer Tecellisi*, (Çev. Nebi Mehdiyev), İstanbul: İnsan Yayınları.

Sönmez, Zeki (1988). *Mimar Sinan İle İlgili Yazmalar-Belgeler*, İstanbul: Mimar Sinan Üniversitesi Yayınları.

Sönmez, Ekizler Serap ve Doğanay, Aziz (2015). "Mimar Sinan Camilerinde Kare ve Altıgen Kurgulu Geometrik Desenler ve Analiz Yöntemleri", *Türk-İslam Medeniyeti Akademik Araştırmalar Dergisi*, S: 19, s. 87-108.

Sönmez, Zekiye (2002). "İnciller ve Kuran Işığında Hz. İsa", *III. Dinler Tarihi Araştırmaları Sempozyumu (9-10 Haziran 2001) Bildirileri*, Ankara: Dinler Tarihi Derneği Yayınları, s. 137-166.

Sözer, Onay (2019). *Sanat: Görünendeki Görünmeyen*, İstanbul: YKY.

Steinsland, Gro (2015). "Tanrılar ve Dev Kadınların Çocukları Olarak Yöneticiler: Pagan Kuzey Yöneticilerin Mitolojisi Üzerine", *Viking Dünyası*, (Ed. Stefan Brink ve Neil Priece), (Çev. Ebru Kılıç), İstanbul: Alfa Yayınları, s. 281-289.

Strano, Giorgio (2018). "Mısır'da Astronomi", *Antik Yakın Doğu*, (Ed. Umberto Eco), (Çev. Leyla Tonguç Basmacı), İstanbul: Alfa Yayınları, s. 453-460.

Şenel, Alaeddin (2019). *İnsanlık Tarihi*, İstanbul: İmge Kitabevi.

Tatar, Burhanettin (2016). *3 Derste Hermenötik*, İstanbul: Vadi Yayınları.

Tillich, Paul (1951). *Systematic Theology*, Vol. 1, Chicago: The University Of Chicago Press.

Tuğrul, Saime (2010). *Ebedi Kutsal Ezeli Kurban*, İstanbul: İletişim Yayınları.

Tuğrul, Saime (2014). *Canım Sana Feda Yeni Zamanların Kutsallık Biçimleri*, İstanbul: İletişim Yayınları.

Tunalı, İsmail (2014). *Sanat Ontolojisi*, İstanbul: İnkılap Yayınevi.

Underhill, Evelyn (2003). *Mysticism: A Study in the Nature and Development of Man's Spiritual Consciousness*, Grand Rapids: Christian Classics Ethereal Library.

Ünalan, Öner (1997). *Darwin Ne Yaptı*, İstanbul: SAYPA Yayınevi.

Winston, Robert (2010). *Tanrının Öyküsü*, (Çev. Sinen Köseoğlu), İstanbul: Say Yayınları.

Xenophon (1994). *Memorabilia*, (Çev. Amy L. Bonnette), London and Ithaka: Cornell University Press.

Yediyıldız, Bahaeddin (1982). "Vakıf Maddesi", *MEB İslam Ansiklopedisi*, C: 13, İstanbul: Milli Eğitim Basımevi, s.153-172.

Yerasimos, Stefanos (2014). *Türk Metinlerinde Konstantiniye ve Ayasofya Efsaneleri*, İstanbul: İletişim Yayınları.

Yıldırım, Nimet (2008). *Fars Mitolojisi Sözlüğü*, İstanbul: Kabalcı Yayınevi.

Yıldırım, Nimet (2012). *İran Mitolojisi*, İstanbul: Pinhan Yayınları.

Yılmaz, Muzaffer (2018). Doğu'dan Batı'ya Bir Yorumlama Denemesi Olarak Babasız Doğma Fenomeni ve Sanat İlişkisi, *22. Uluslararası Ortaçağ ve Türk Dönemi Kazıları ve Sanat Tarihi Araştırmaları Sempozyumu (24-26 Ekim 2019) Özet Kitabı*, İstanbul: MSGSÜ Yayınları.

Yılmaz, Muzaffer (2018). "Batı Resminde Yeme-İçme Konulu Sahnelerin Menşei Üzerine Bir Değerlendirme (Ortaçağ'ın Başlangıcından Barok Dönemin Sonuna Kadar)", *SDÜ Fen-Edebiyat Fakültesi Sosyal Bilimler Dergisi,* S: 44, s. 111-138.

Yüksek, Hasan (2006). "Anadolu Selçuklularında Vakıflar", *Anadolu Selçukluları ve Beylikler Dönemi Uygarlığı I,* Ankara: Kültür ve Turizm Bakanlığı Yayınları, s. 309-325.

Online

Holy Quran
https://kuran.diyanet.gov.tr/

Tanakh and Bible
https://www.kutsalkitap.org/

www.ingramcontent.com/pod-product-compliance
Lightning Source LLC
LaVergne TN
LVHW050141080526
838202LV00062B/6546